AF008473

THE JUDGE, THE GAVEL, & THE GUN - TAMING NEBRASKA'S WILD FRONTIER

By Roy V. Alleman and Carol L. Nowka

Publisher:

Nebraska Wealth.com

Cover Illustration

Design by Susan Snyder of PCS Training.net

Editor

Ellen Campbell

Pictures on front cover:

Judge Gaslin, a drawing created by Omaha World Herald
Permission granted by John Haskell,
author of **Judge William Gaslin – Nebraska Jurist**

Doc Middleton, First Custer county Court House and
I.P. (Print) Olive, Photographer S.D. Butcher and
provided by the Nebraska State Historical Society
Photograph Collections.

Library of Congress Control #200627600

Copyright: © 2005 by Carol L. Nowka

No part of this book may be reproduced or transmitted
in any form or by any means, graphic, electronic, or
mechanical, including photocopying, recording, taping
or by any information storage retrieval system,
without the written permission of the publisher.

ISBN 0-9746206-2-9
Second edition

Printed in the United States of America

Lighting Source. Com

Contents

Chapter One	The West – An Eye Opener - 1873	 7
Chapter Two	Setting the Stage – The "New West"	... 15
Chapter Three	Starting Over Again - 1874	... 21
Chapter Four	The "Hanging Judge" - 1875	... 28
Chapter Five	The Olive "Gang" - 1876	... 33
Chapter Six	The Farmer and the Cowman Don't Mix - 1877	... 36
Chapter Seven	Early Frontier Justice - 1878	... 51
Chapter Eight	Reining in the Frontier	... 64
Chapter Nine	The Gavel and the Gun -1879	... 71
Chapter Ten	Justice is Served	... 88
Chapter Eleven	Doc Middleton – A Notorious Outlaw or a Hopeless Romantic?	... 92
Chapter Twelve	Doc Middleton and the Gun Battle at Long Pine - 1880	... 97
Chapter Thirteen	Appeals court – an Outrageous Decision	...104
Chapter Fourteen	Judge Gaslin's Circus of Circuits - 1881	...109
Chapter Fifteen	Law of a Different Kind	...120
Chapter Sixteen	Is The Frontier Conquered? 1882	...126
Chapter Seventeen	The Judge and his Great Nephew	...134
Bibliography		...144
About the Authors		...145

Acknowledgements

I am extremely grateful to my father, Roy V. Alleman who was a great storyteller and author. He wrote the original manuscript for this story, based upon actual news articles of the time and a biography written by the Judge's great nephew, John Haskell.

My father originally called his story "The Taming of Nebraska's Frontier". At his age of 90 he was in the process of finding a publisher, when he died. But to that day, he was always thinking about stories to write and really enjoyed reading history and the telling of Nebraska historical tales.

My father's previous books, both true stories, were **Blizzard 1949** and **The Bloody Saga of White Rock**. Both books can be purchased from any retail store or from NebraskaWealth.com.

I am also grateful to Ellen Campbell, the editor and her encouragement. I, never having written a book before, was reticent about my ability to take this story and improve upon it and make it ready for publication. But as all authors witness, I did it, but not without a lot of help. I also wish to acknowledge Grand Island, Nebraska Writer's Network. They allowed me to see the struggles, but the almighty dream of writing a book.

Co-author Carol L. Nowka

I dedicate this work to my father and mother, who always said

"You can do it."

A wise king stamps out crime by severe punishment.

Prov. 20:26 --- The Living Bible

CHAPTER ONE

The West – An Eye Opener

1873

That spring two covered wagons trekked up the east side of the Middle Loup River, crossing it 20 miles north of Loup City and stopped overnight with Custer County's first homesteading family, the Dowses. Ami Ketchum drove one wagon, Luther Mitchell the other accompanied by his wife and stepdaughter, Tamar Snow, a pretty young lass engaged to Ami.

"We have come from St. Paul, Nebraska, and we're hunting for new lands," said Mitchell after supper, "We're veterans of the War, serving with the North. We thought you might help us find the best site.

"You could find good land nearby but there is excellent land in the Clear Creek Valley southwest of here also in Custer County," said Dowse. "It's unsettled for the most part giving you a choice of the best. But there's a big cow outfit out there and it's sometimes a battle to keep their cattle out of crops. Print, Bob and Ira Olive run the outfit.

"Rumor has it that ranchers sometimes pay for the crops if their cattle break down fences and destroy crops. But I've also heard of cowboys cutting barbwire fences and letting cattle and horses in. The Olives are Texans and, I have heard, they are hot headed and quick to use a gun."

Mitchell didn't say much. Ketchum, quickly assured Dowse he was a crack shot with a rifle or revolver. "We have a right to protect ourselves. They've no legal right to the land."

"I like the sound of Clear Creek but we don't want trouble," added the more cautious Mitchell.

"Squatter's right has long been a part of our land ownership." said Dowse. "One young cowboy said, 'We were here first.' But using a million acres, to me, hardly qualifies as squatter's right. You may be right but don't be dead right," he cautioned Ami. This foreboding of events to come, fell on deaf ears to these two young men – Ami Ketchum and Luther Mitchell.

Therein were the beginnings of the settling of Nebraska Territory, rich land, lots of land, many uses for the land, cowboys, Indians and the farmers – a great mix for trouble and no law to be seen for miles.

Draw a line north and south midway through the new state of Nebraska in 1868, when William Gaslin and wife Catherine came from Maine, one will find east of the line getting fairly well settled with more homesteaders moving in to put down roots on each quarter section of land. Villages were being established as well as law and order with courts. Railroads were under construction.

But west of that line, from Kearney on, in the area stretching 300 west and 100 miles north and south---well, that is a different story.

Nebraska became a state the year before, carved from Nebraska Territory. A legislature was elected. A legislative committee, with little to go by, drew lines on a map to mark out counties in the western half and named them. This committee gave little thought to mundane matters such as county government, courthouses and judges. The county officials of these counties, when settled, would have to do that.

Population grew along the Union Pacific Railroad as it followed the Platte River into Wyoming and points west. A few homesteaders dared to move into the Republican River Valley on the south but many, including attorney William Gaslin, a newcomer from Maine were often scared out by the Indian tribes of Kansas.

Otherwise, this land was inhabited mostly by mighty herds of cattle and the cowboys who branded calves in the spring and held fall roundups to gather grass-fat steers for shipment to Chicago. Herds of buffalo still competed with cattlemen for the available grass.

Except in a few counties along the Platte River there was little law and order. Lawless characters took full advantage and found it a safe place to steal and commit crime. There was variety in these characters. Some came here one jump ahead of a sheriff of an eastern state. Others came from Texas for the same reason. A few came earlier to avoid the Civil War draft, both north and south.

Among the outlaws were Jesse and Frank James, the Younger brothers, and Kid Wade who found it safe to rob new banks or wherever there was money. Sam Bass later would rob the Union Pacific Railroad and get away with it.

The Gaslins, before coming from Maine, had carefully read the Union Pacific bulletins but what they found when they arrived in Omaha was not exactly what they expected in this new land. They came discouraged and broke when they checked into an Omaha hotel in the muddy spring of 1868. Their depressed feelings were not helped much as they listened to the sounds on the street. Cursing and swearing drifted up through the window as men delivered supplies and more barrels of liquor to the many saloons. They heard a few gunshots and more profanity, which annoyed Catherine very much.

But doing something about the high crime rate in the new state or even right here in Omaha, was not a high priority with attorney Gaslin then.

Life had never been easy for William Gaslin. Right now he felt life had dealt him a "bad hand", in fact, several bad hands. He was born near China, Maine, on July 29, 1827, the eldest of five children. There was never enough food on the table and so, at 16, Gaslin went to work as a shoveler on a millrace, and with that money, purchased a rocky farm for his parents.

He worked as a sailor and at other jobs until he had enough money to attend Kent High School. At 25, he graduated from Bowdoin College with a Bachelor of Arts degree. He secured a law degree and went into business in Augusta, Maine.

His first client, a poor old widow, was being robbed of her farm and home due to a flaw in the title. The best lawyers advised him he could do nothing for her but he determined to try. The court granted him a delay and he spent most of the summer examining records, looking for a detail in the title that might favor his client. Finally he found the detail and won the case. She gave all the money she had for his services--$2.50. The case established his reputation and he never wanted for clients. However, in 1865, a fire hit the city and consumed his office.

He and Catherine Perkins were married in 1866. A son, born a year later, died in infancy. Catherine was devastated with grief and they decided to go west. They landed in Omaha in 1868, a year after Nebraska achieved statehood and a year before the Union Pacific Railroad finished crossing the nation. For Nebraska, it was a time of transition from the wild and woolly west to an organized government of law and order; from huge cattle outfits, cowboys and Indians to settled farms and smaller ranches. Nebraska judicial districts were fully established in eastern Nebraska but none for the western half of the state. The eastern half of the state was mostly settled, and the western half was beginning to settle rapidly as more and more homesteaders trekked west to file claims on raw, unbroken prairie.

An unhappy wife was not a good way to start in a new land. There was mud on the floor and on some on their clothes from the carriage's spinning wheels. William Gaslin tried to comfort his wife, without much success.

"I'll find us a house away from all of this tomorrow," he promised.

"Oh, I hope so," exclaimed Catherine.

The Gaslins were not a well-matched couple physically. She was dark haired, slim and beautiful. She was as tall as he, maybe taller. He was pudgy, round faced with squinty eyes, certainly not handsome. He was quiet, meditative, and moved rather deliberately. He was no mortal for show, and would remove his tie and coat for comfort whether they had company or not. She was the active sort, always ready for some fun. That is she was until they lost their only child, a beautiful son. The stress of these differences and the grief she suffered caused her to feel the entitlement to complaining and or nagging. Adding additional difficulty to their lives.

Gaslin did find a livable home at the edge of town although it took a while. Omaha, being a new town with a building boom, made homes for rent hard to find and expensive.

He put up his business sign, but finding clients was slow work.

"I am not doing well as an attorney," he had to admit.

However, he also admitted he wouldn't take criminal cases until he was sure they were innocent, and there weren't many of this type. This year alone, the city of Omaha tried 75 men for murder.

One day he came home to report he had another job. He told Catherine "I have been hired by the Nebraska State Board of Immigration, to go up the Republican River Valley and bring back information regarding soil, grass, habitation and crops that can be used to lure potential settlers from the East to Nebraska.

"When I get through, I may find a community that's better suited to us and more civilized than here. I hope you won't mind being alone for a short time." To which Catherine did not reply.

The next morning a man pulled up with mule teams and two wagons for the journey. Gaslin joined him, driving one team.

He wrote to Catherine and sent the letters back whenever he met a traveler going east. Portions were such as these:

> "Tuesday, July 11. After an early breakfast, started across a very level country. No wood, nor water. In Nuckolls and Webster Counties we passed but one house. Camped at a creek for dinner. Arrived at Francis that night, where we remained through July 12 and 13. Feasted ourselves on buffalo, two having been caught just as we arrived. Land here is poor and broken but little timbered."

Or,

> "Friday, July 14. Traveled over one of the most broken and worthless sections of country I have ever seen in Nebraska. Soil too sandy, and little timber. Thompson Creek very broken and west of it for some distance, about four miles or better, soil more even. Fine site for a town. The day is hot."

The next day, July 15, they entered Harlan County and Gaslin changed his opinion of the country. The valley was wide with fine clumps of timber. They encountered vast herds of buffalo.

In fact, Gaslin liked the country so well he and a partner, Herman Leisinger, each homesteaded a quarter section of land and proceeded to build a sod house on the line between their lands. He made the commitment to living on it three years before he could "prove up", as required by the Homestead Act of 1862. The homesteaders had to prove they had lived on the land so many years, plowed so many acres of land, and build a home. Then they would be given ownership after paying a small fee.

He wrote glowing descriptive letters:

> "You'll love this pretty valley. Wait until I build a log cabin and get settled. Wait until you hear the wild turkeys gobble and the whip-poor-

wills call! My neighbor, Herman Leisinger, and I are building near each other on our adjoining land."

Catherine was not impressed.

"You're an attorney, and a good one," she sent back, "and you should be practicing it, not chasing buffalo calves, as you described in your recent letter".

He had written her about how they caught a buffalo calf and taught him to eat corn. It was true, as she pointed out, there was plenty of need for lawyers on the frontier around Lowell and Kearney north, and points west. Stories coming down from there indicated criminals were getting away with murder, thievery and all sorts of crime. One favorite trick so often heard was how criminals bluffed out the judge.

All packed six shooters on their hips and carried rifles in saddle scabbards. All were crack shots and sure to strike terror into the hearts of local law officers. Sometimes the federal government sent out U. S. Marshals, which didn't seem to scare the outlaws much.

If an outlaw were hailed into a frontier court his friends packed the courtroom, pearl-handled guns flashing. They let it be known that nothing "better happen to their friend." The judge usually wilted and declared the man "not guilty," much to the disgust of good citizens and most especially to Gaslin. It worked for the most part, unless angry citizens formed a vigilante committee and took the law into their own hands. Then the outlaw might find himself hanged to the nearest cottonwood tree, telegraph cross arms, or crudely constructed gallows.

It always happened in local courts since western Nebraska was not yet in any judicial district. Gaslin often discussed this unhappy state of affairs with Leisinger and with Catherine in letters.

Three years after filing and Catherine still living in Omaha, he had title to his homestead. Now, he was a landowner in a new state. His legal title called it the south half of the south half of section 23, township two, and range 19, Orleans Township. He was excited that the time had passed so quickly and he was finally a landowner. Catherine was not so sure.

Renegade Sioux Indians were harassing settlers in southwestern Nebraska and northwestern Kansas, causing many settlers to leave. Some had been killed. One day the Blue family came through and told their story as to why they were moving to Lowell.

Blue's 14-year-old son, Clark, late in the spring, rode to a neighbor's place a mile away to get seed corn. He noticed the neighbor boy herding cattle on horseback and at about the same time he saw Indians riding over a hill. The boy took for cover as fast as his horse could take him but it was not fast enough. The Indians caught him and killed him with a tomahawk to the head.

Clark was stunned, but he quickly rode to the neighbor's house as fast as he could with the Indians on his tail. He ran into the house, slammed and locked the door behind him. "Indians!" he yelled to the lone woman in house.

The house was half dugout and half sod with a sod roof. The Indians came screaming and yelling. They climbed on the roof and proceeded to tear off chunks to get in.

The housewife offered him a rifle. "Here, take this. I'll make more bullets."

The Indians tore a hole about two feet square in the roof. When one of them stuck his head over the hole to look inside, Clark blew part of his head off with the big slug in the rifle. The other Indians dragged the man from the roof and left.

"We're moving to Lowell where we think it is safer," Blue told Gaslin.

One day Leisinger and Gaslin drove to Lowell, the nearest land office, to file their homestead claims. Gaslin was impressed with the thriving village.

"Good place to have an office if I were of a mind to return to law," he told Leisinger. "But I like it where we are."

While drinking coffee at the new hotel, Gaslin met J. Dilworth, a Kearney attorney.

"This land is settling up fast and I don't see why the state doesn't establish a district court out here," said Dilworth. "The governor doesn't realize how fast we're getting populated. Our county courts are weak and many counties don't yet even have a courthouse. Criminals get away with murder. Angry settlers want to take the law in their own hands. You ought to get back into practicing law."

"Someday, maybe, but not now," said Gaslin.

However, there had been a severe turn in the weather, with a couple of terrible snowstorms and many cattle herds frozen to death. It ended the prevailing belief that this country would always have mild winters. It also ended Gaslin's infatuation with farm life.

He wrote Catherine: "I'm moving to Lowell. Join me there. I am going to begin my practice by helping the settlers with their land grant applications."

She packed up what they had and caught the first passenger train heading west.

Judge Gaslin and clients in law office.

Courtesy John Haskell

Gaslin formed a law partnership with N. S. Morlan in Lowell in 1872. They had a growing business helping new settlers "prove up" on homesteads. He rented an apartment in a large hotel in Lowell. Catherine and he moved in at once. How nice to be together again. They had been separated for nearly four years.

CHAPTER TWO

Setting the Stage – The "New West"

1873

From his law office right next door to the stylish Continental Hotel, William Gaslin could see most of Lowell, Nebraska. There, on the tracks south of town, a train with a long string of stock cars, patiently waited, its engines puffing gently.

Cowboys, noisily and profanely, herded cattle into the corrals and on into the cars to await shipment east. The horns of the longhorn steers clacked against the wooden doors as they twisted their necks to accommodate the narrow openings. The crack of a bullwhip changed the minds of non-cooperating steers. Gaslin's view was hampered by clouds of dust rising from the trampling of a thousand hoofs.

On the prairie south and east of town, more herds waited their turn at the corrals. It was September 1873, the time of year when vast herds arrived from Texas to be shipped east to either be butchered or fattened in the feedlots.

Two cowboys relieved of herd duty rode down Main Street at a full gallop, whooping and shooting into the air, pistols held high. Gaslin watched, fascinated, as they slid their horses to a halt in front of a saloon and stomped in, spurs jangling on the boardwalk.

Swirling dust caked the sides of the sweating horses as they waited for men to return.

The rail tracks, recently built by Burlington and Missouri Railroad south of the Platte River, were the end of this line for now. Lowell came into existence immediately to accommodate the anticipated business.

Gaslin looked with pride on the bustling community. Across the street sat the new courthouse; down the street business fronts were painted bright colors. There were blacksmith shops, general merchandise stores, hairdressers, barbershops, and others.

Seven saloons, though it was mid-morning, were busy accommodating thirsty cowboys and gamblers. Dealers at the gaming tables were doing their best to separate young herdsmen from the pay they received at the end of the cattle drive. He could hear a tinkling piano. He should get back to work but it was hot inside as well as outside. He needed a breath of fresh air, nearly choking on the dust which dimmed his view of the sand hills west and south, and the great herds grazing there waiting their turn at the pens. For once the wind wasn't blowing. It was all so exciting and he didn't want to miss anything.

Gaslin thought he heard a gunshot but it was muffled by the deafening sounds of the street and the stockyards. Main Street was busy as drivers of drays picked up loads at the new depot and unloaded at the stores, Homesteaders in wagons covered with crude canvas that hid their scant worldly possessions stopped for supplies or to file homestead claims. Gaslin and Morlan waited for them to show up at their office.

He was not so sure Catherine shared his excitement. "I'll never get used to all that profanity and crude language," she said, "I'll bet most of the young men came from good homes in Texas."

Lowell was typical of the shipping points that shifted west each year as new rail lines built into the frontier. In Kansas and Nebraska settlers took land previously grazed by the herds.

"Herdsmen better enjoy this circus," Gaslin told Morlan. "It isn't going to last long. Changes are coming fast."

"But we'll enjoy it while it lasts," added Morlan as he assisted a new home seeker with his claim papers.

Gaslin and Morlan were too busy to spend much time in meditation. Helping homesteaders kept them and six other lawyers in monetary clover in Lowell.

For the first time in a long while, life was pleasant for Catherine and William Gaslin. They enjoyed living here, spending evenings dining at the Continental Hotel and eating with elegant and costly silverware.

There were frequent dances at the Continental ballroom. Catherine loved to dance and was popular with the men, so many of whom were single. William was not all that interested in dancing and would rather sit at a table and enjoy a glass of wine with a fellow attorney. His favorite was C. J. Dilworth who, like Gaslin, had strong convictions about law and order - or in the case of Lowell, the lack of it.

Otherwise, Gaslin liked to go to the Lowell Register, the local newspaper and pick up exchange papers to see what was going on in the rest of the state. An article in the North Platte Advertiser held his interest. It indicated why cattlemen weren't really ready yet to give up the open and free range. It praised Nebraska rangeland, its excellent grass and bountiful supply of good water. It also praised the winters, and how cattle grazed all winter with no supplemental hay or grain.

"I think the editor better remember the big "die-up" (cattle losses) of past winters when blizzards howled across the country," Gaslin told the editor.

"These cattlemen hate to give up their free range," said the editor. "They would like to hold back the homesteaders any way possible even, though they know they can't. They're behind the "fence" law passed by the Nebraska legislature which will compel these settlers to fence their fields."

"It will be a bone of contention for years to come, and drive judges crazy. These longhorn cattle don't have much respect for fences anyway," said Gaslin.

"It's exciting to be part of the developing western part of this state," he told Catherine over supper. She wasn't particularly impressed.

"Too much blood and thunder," she answered.

Catherine was right. Bad liquor or too much of it often got Texas cowboys into a pack of trouble. There was the story of John Smith who killed a young farmer over horses in his care, which had gotten into the farmer's cornfield. The recounting of it had people in an angry uproar. The story goes that one evening the monotony of herding 60 or 70 head of horses north of the new Platte River Bridge, south of Kearney was too much for John Smith and several other Texas cowboys. Smith suggested they ride into Kearney for a drink. "How about the horses" asked one? "They're close to that corn field." "They'll be all right," said Smith, "Plenty of grazing. We'll be back before dark. Besides, the boss says with the new fence law, we don't have to worry about corn fields."

Maybe their intentions were good but it was the next morning before the men returned, their common sense confused by liquor. In the meantime the horses invaded Milton Collins' cornfield. When they rode out of town they saw their horses in Collins' corral. Milton was on his horse and stationed at the gate. He was unarmed. The other men hesitated but Smith rode up and demanded the horses be turned out. "I won't let them go until you pay me $20 damages," replied Collins.

"You let those horses out and don't you say a word, or I'll..."

Frightened, Milton jumped off his horse and ran to the house. Smith fired his six-shooter and Milton dropped dead just as he reached the door. Smith and company opened the corral gate and headed the horses south across the bridge.

Milton, a young man, lived with his new wife and his father, Asbury, on the farm. He was proud of that cornfield, his first, and anticipated a good harvest. Now it was in shambles and he lay dead.

Asbury rode to town and quickly rounded up a posse. He also telegraphed Sheriff Games of Dawson, the next county west. There, U. S. Deputy Marshall John E. Roe and D. B. Ball organized a posse of 15 men and headed east to corner the men from that direction. By evening they surrounded the men in a sand blowout southwest of Kearney. All of the men except Smith surrendered. Smith was captured the next morning near the Platte River Bridge.

By that time the story had traveled all over the country around Lowell and Kearney. People were outraged. The Collins family was highly respected, and Asbury had been a probate judge.

"They'll be brought to trial," Gaslin told Catherine, "if they can keep the mob from hanging them first."

"Can't the sheriff stop them?" asked Catherine.

"No problem usually. They just break the jail door and take them. I'll be at the trial along with C. J. Dilworth,"

Smith was charged with murder. Two cohorts, Mathew and Mitchell, were charged with shooting at Collins. They denied it and were released, the evidence convincing the judge they were telling the truth.

At the trial in Kearney Gaslin and Dilworth found seats up

front in the Buffalo County courtroom.

First witness, D. A. Crowel, described the details of the murder. Others confirmed his testimony. The defense attorneys offered little in rebuttal. The jury, with little sympathy for the criminal, acted quickly to convict Smith of second-degree murder. The judge sentenced him to life in prison.

"Who knows? Maybe the law is gaining a little respect in this part of the state after all," whispered Gaslin to Dilworth.

However Gaslin spoke too quickly. The defense attorneys, appearing before the three-judge Nebraska Supreme Court, argued successfully and Smith was set free. Wisely, he left the state for parts unknown.

"The damned Supreme Court," snorted Gaslin the next time he met Dilworth. "This is a good example of miscarriage of justice so common in this part of the state. No wonder people resort to mob rule and vigilante committees."

Most often the troubles were a matter of too many guns mixed with too much rotgut whiskey. In one case, what might have been just a good fist fight turned into a bloody shooting spree. A group of cowboys and renegades were drinking in a Lowell saloon. One from each group started a fight and the rest joined in. When the smoke cleared, six young men lay dead plus a saloon girl who died trying to escape. Three men lay wounded. All seven of the dead were buried in Boot Hill Cemetery east of town, so called because most of those buried there died with their boots on.

Gaslin sat in on a trial in Lowell that charged a man with needless murder. Friends of the accused came with six-shooters on their hips and glared at the judge and prosecuting attorney. The judge wilted and called it self-defense. Gaslin watched with disgust, nudging the pistol in a holster hanging at his side.

"If I had been judge the outcome would have been different," he told his partner.

"Who knows, you might get your chance," answered Morlan.

Even horse thieves didn't let the law worry them too much. Gaslin bought a beautiful white mare for Catherine, planning to buy her a sidesaddle. Then she could ride around Lowell and enjoy herself, doing something besides dancing. Someone stole the little mare. He reported it to Sheriff Dave Anderson of Kearney. Nothing came of it.

Citizens of Kearney County voted Minden the county seat instead of Lowell. The Union Pacific Railroad, now completed through Nebraska, would take much of the rail traffic from Lowell. With settlers crowding west, the cattle shipping point would move to Ogallala. All this would bring an end to Lowell's prosperity. Gaslin disliked the lawlessness of Lowell. He felt Bloomington would become the county seat of Franklin County, and was considering moving there. Also, Catherine and he were not getting along well. After a dance late one night Catherine told him she wanted a divorce.

"Why? Do you want to marry that handsome attorney you dance with so much?"

"Yes, that is what I will do."

"Then I am moving to Bloomington."

Catherine and Gaslin went through a devastating divorce that left both of them very bitter.

"Maybe it was my fault," Gaslin confessed to Morlan. "I left her alone so much and she must have been terribly lonesome for companionship."

"Is that why you're moving to Bloomington?" Morlan asked, as Gaslin waited for the buggy that would haul his meager possessions.

"One reason, maybe. But this town will die on the vine when the county seat is moved to Minden. Kearney will become the main city on the river. Farmers will push the cattlemen west so this will no longer be a shipping point.

"Will you water that little cottonwood I just planted out front?" He added," I pulled it up yesterday as I drove in, and used it to swat my horse. I thought it might grow and give you shade someday. By the way, Dilworth says we may become a part of the new Fifth Judicial District at the next session of the legislature."

Rearranging the tie that hung loosely around the neck of his once-white shirt, he lifted his frame and looked out the window to see if the buggy was coming. He carried a bucket of water to the sapling.

(Thirty years later he would return to see this sapling had grown into a 40-foot spreading shade tree, about all that was left of Lowell.)

CHAPTER THREE

Starting Over Again

1874

As Gaslin drove south over the sandy, rolling hills, he let the team pick its way along the trail that led to Bloomington. Longhorn steers contentedly grazed the luxurious grass, barely getting out of the way, their long horns clacking occasionally against the iron tires of the buggy wheels. Cowboys circled each herd, riding at a lope or trot, careful the cattle didn't mix. He could still hear the noise at the stockyards where cattle were being loaded. It was September and the last of the trail herds were coming in.

A warm breeze blew from the south. Meadowlarks sang from perches on long stems of the yucca plants, antelope stared curiously from a nearby hill. It was a wonderful day, one to be enjoyed. However, its beauty was lost on William Gaslin. He was too depressed. He stared at his shoes and was soon lost in deep thought as he reviewed his past and pondered his future.

After much contemplation, he decided to rent office space in Bloomington, but his business began with a slow start.

One day about mid-afternoon, William Gaslin propped his feet on the desk of his law office and heaved a sigh of satisfied relief. He had just settled a dispute over a boundary between a client and his neighbor that was getting heated. Gaslin suggested they find the quarter section surveyor stakes, line-sight the boundary line and agree to the results. They did so and had just left his office, good friends again. He didn't make much money but it gave him a lot of satisfaction. The case gave him a sense of optimism for his future and the future of the town.

The main street of his new town was lined with buggies, covered wagons and buckboards; their owners were there to file on a claim at the land office or to stock up on supplies and groceries.

A few cow ponies tied up at the hitching rail switched their tails and shooed flies as they waited for their owners to come back. There weren't many. The annual fall roundup was on and most cowboys were out of town. Gaslin could hear the shrill whine of the water-powered sawmill near the river as it cut slabs from a cottonwood log. An energetic newcomer had just finished a millrace and installed a water wheel. Across the street he could hear the thump-thump of the press as the <u>Bloomington Guard</u> rolled out its latest edition. He would walk over soon and get a copy. A homesteader walked in, seeking help with his claim.

Land seekers were his chief clients as the tide of homesteaders moved west. His reputation for being a fair but competent attorney followed him from Lowell. His law practice helped take away the pain of losing Catherine to a once-friendly attorney in Lowell. It was hard to believe he had lost her. He thought they were beginning to have a pretty good life together.

At the <u>Bloomington Guard</u> office he thumbed exchange papers from equally new frontier newspapers. From them he learned not all was quiet on the frontier. Feelings often ran high between cattlemen and settlers; between cattlemen and the horse thieves and cattle rustlers; between everyone and the murderous men who came to the frontier one jump ahead of the law somewhere else.

There was one more factor in all this. The nation was still divided by the Civil War even though it officially ended nine years before. Cattlemen usually came from Texas and the south. Homesteaders often came from northern states, but southern states as well. It didn't take much to trigger a fight. Reporters wrote of all this in excellent detail. Often the editor put in his personal opinion, which could be dangerous for him.

Gaslin returned that afternoon to the newspaper editor's back shop reading the exchange papers and the articles the editor had reprinted in the paper.

An article copied from the <u>North Platte Advertiser</u> drew his interest. It emphasized the contrast between the new and the disappearing old frontier:

> "Buffalo in front of you, buffalo to the right of you, buffalo to the left of you---and thus did the fifty thousand bison charge down from the hills and canyons and fill all the Platte Valley on the south side of the Platte River Thursday and Friday last."

The buffalo filled the valley west of town. The editor called the landscape black with the animals. Everyone with a horse and rifle left to get his buffalo,

Men got plenty of meat and then, for excitement, began roping calves. The article related a story about a man by the name of Brady, nicknamed "Old Soda." He got dumped to the ground when the bull calf he roped charged between his horse's legs, adding to the hilarity of the occasion.

The editor urged people to come out, as this might be their last chance to hunt the "Monarch of the Plains." "The numbers of buffalo in this herd are variously estimated from ten to fifty thousand." He wrote, "The sight is one not often to be enjoyed and will be still less in the future because the bison, like the Indians, are fast disappearing from the Great American Desert."

"What a way to study the history of the Plains," Gaslin told the editor. The editor, busy plucking small type from a case with which to print another small article, didn't bother to answer.

Gaslin continued to talk, half to himself, half to the printer. "The editor is right. This life style won't last much longer. But he is not wise to encourage cattlemen. Sure, it's a good life for now. No taxes, no lease or rent, nor ownership of the grassland, all free.

"Sure, last winter was mild but can't they remember past winters when they had huge 'die-ups'? But if they think they can stop the steady march of the homesteaders, they better think again. That new 'fence law' they finagled through the legislature requiring that if a farmer doesn't want cattle in his fields he has to fence them won't help. Just cause more fights. The farmers will fence their cornfields with or without a law.

"There will be clashes, mark my word. You know, the irresistible force that meets an immovable object. There will be a horrible crash before this is over and settled," predicted Gaslin.

The printer just kept on with his type setting, never looking up as Gaslin left the print shop.

Reading the <u>Lexington Observer</u>, from a copy in the print shop dated June 13, 1874, Gaslin learned that one set of outlaws hopefully might not bother Nebraska for a while; the Younger brothers had moved to Texas. It appeared that, while robbing a bank in Plum Creek[*], perhaps they shot Deputy Sheriff McDaniels

---

[*] Current day Lexington

of Dawson County. The editor wrote:

> "We had a telegram from John S. Barnhill, for many years a citizen of Wellington, Texas, well known to everybody in the west end of Lafayette County and now a resident of Sherman, Texas. He informs us that he met with the Younger boys in that city two weeks ago (May 5).
> The Younger brothers, Cole, Bob and Jim, arrived there on Monday night, May 4, and registered at the Southern Hotel. Tuesday morning, learning that he (Barnhill) was living in the city, they sought him out and spent an hour or so in his office...."

The men appeared to be moving to Mexico to enjoy their ill-gotten gain and seemed to expect Barnhill to relay the message to Nebraska. They and Barnhill had served together in the Confederate Army. Or, did they want to throw off the lawmen in Nebraska in case they did return?

Jim Younger expressed regret for killing McDaniels, but insisted it was self-defense, "He was a good man and a Confederate soldier."

"We're glad to get rid of them," added the editor. "We hope they find congenial pastimes in revolutionary Mexico, sufficient to give them employment for the balance of their lives."

Two Younger brothers, Bud and John, had been killed in brushes with the law, maybe in Nebraska bank robberies. The Plum Creek editor said they worked in cahoots with the James brothers at times. He said he was not sure of this except that many people said they had seen the James boys in Nebraska, even in Lowell."

William Gaslin made a few notes about these men under the heading of "Men to be watched." He continued his notes with "Hanging or shooting is the surest way to control hardened outlaws. It hurts to see good lawmen shot down by these criminals."

From the Sidney newspaper Gaslin read an exiting account of a cowboy's escapade there. It would also illustrate how young men sometimes get into crime without seeking it.

It appeared, according to this article, that a young man named Harrington and his boss, James Bryce, a freighter to the Black Hills, sat in a corner of a saloon in Sidney, listlessly listening to a man beat out popular tunes on a piano. Their wagons were loaded and they would get an early start the next morning.

Soldiers from the nearby fort were drinking and threatening to cause trouble. One of them approached Harrington and said, "I heard you say you can whip any SOB that wears the Blue."

"Not me, But I can take you to the man who did say that."

"Then do."

Harrington ushered the soldier to the man who promptly hauled off and knocked the soldier to the floor. Returning to his chair near Bryce a lieutenant struck him, knocking him to the floor. Before he could rise, other soldiers kicked him and volleyed blows on him. Bryce ran to help his friend but before he could get there Harrington drew his revolvers, shot the lieutenant dead and wounded several others. Harrington ran out and hid in a culvert. The soldiers proceeded to shoot up the town, and rampaged until the cavalry rode in and tamed them down.

Harrington made his way to the Bryce camp and waited for Bryce. When he returned, they planned to leave for the Black Hills, but Bryce said, "I urge you turn yourself in. You will never be convicted, and you can clear your name."

Harrington wavered. "I don't believe I would ever get a fair trial. Did you ever try taking on the U. S. government? Especially if you are from the South?"

Bryce tried harder but Harrington never turned himself in to the sheriff.

Perhaps, there was more to it. Gaslin learned from the printer that Harrington was an alias, that he had joined a trail herd under another name and his father had been hanged for stealing horses. Harrington was a handsome young man, tall, wiry and slender with deep-set, piercing eyes. "He showed he could handle his six shooters," said the printer of the paper, whose sympathy for the soldiers was limited.

Bryce told the editor of the Sidney newspaper that Harrington was honest. "I trusted him with $3,500 worth of mules."

"I have a feeling we'll hear more about this young man," Gaslin told the printer. "And not in the best way." Another name to be watched, wrote Gaslin in his ever-ready notebook.

Gaslin's hunch was right. Harrington soon left freighting, changed his name to Doc Middleton and began a career in horse thievery. There were plenty of opportunities. Thousand of horses ran free except for the annual cattle roundups. So why the hatred of horse thieves? In this area larger than some states, the only transportation of importance besides horseflesh was the Union Pacific Railroad that ran through Nebraska. Men rode horses, as well as used them to pull their wagons and buggies. Towns and ranches were far apart. Take a man's horse and you might set him afoot miles from any habitation. A man watched his horses, carefully. Besides, there was a sort of love relationship between a man and his horse. He kept a horse until it died of old age; a privilege not accorded any other farm animal. A cow was butchered or hauled off to market when she got old.

Gaslin watched for reports of Doc Middleton and remembered the white horse he purchased for Catherine that was stolen. Wanted posters appeared in banks and post offices offering rewards for Middleton "dead or alive."

This was just one item that disgusted Gaslin. It was especially upsetting to Gaslin to hear the story of the needless killing of David Vroman who, with his pregnant wife and seven children, had settled southwest of Lowell and constructed a dugout, looking forward to a good life on their homestead in Nebraska. They had moved there in March to plant crops and raise livestock.

On September 7, Vroman and son Thomas saddled up and left in the early morning to tend livestock. "They have drifted too far away," he told his wife. "But we should be back before too long."

Mrs. Vroman cooked a big breakfast, then waited and waited.... Finally when she went out to look for them, she noticed their horses standing about a half mile away. Walking to them she found her husband and son dead. She knelt down between them, and prayed and wept over the bodies. She could see no way to survive without her husband, and take care of seven children and another on the way.

Later it was learned a man by the name of Williams, shot the father and son in an altercation over livestock. She buried her husband and son in Boot Hill Cemetery. She gave birth to another son with the aid of a neighbor, and tried desperately to feed eight mouths. One day when there was no food left in the dugout, she knelt again and prayed desperately. The next morning she stepped out the door to find a sack of flour on her doorstep. It was a "gift from heaven." A neighbor had left it early that morning. Williams was never tried for murder.

"It's a neighborhood squabble but look what it does to this woman left with children and no means of support, Somehow we have to stop these crimes," Gaslin told the editor of the Bloomington Guard. "Williams, or any of these murderers, can easily get lost out there in cow camps and the wild country."

"Maybe you'll get a chance to do something about it," said the editor.

CHAPTER FOUR

The "Hanging Judge"

1875

William Gaslin, opening the telegram that lie on his desk when he came back from dinner, read with considerable interest,
"We'll be nominating judges for the newly organized fifth district and we want you to be our candidate. We hope you will attend the Republican Party Convention in Plum Creek."[*]

He was taken by surprise. He walked south to the edge of the hill and gazed over the beautiful Republican Valley. He could hear the sharp sound of an axe as a settler cut into a log to be used for a cabin. Across the river, cattle winded their way down to the river for water. A prairie chicken boomed in the distance. If he had to live without Catherine, where could he find a better place? He didn't want to leave this valley, but he was the one who said repeatedly he would like an opportunity to strike at the lawless frontier. He walked back to his office and penned a telegram saying he would be there.

****

In 1875 Nebraska adopted a new constitution. It created an independent supreme court, and divided the state into six judicial districts. Judges would be elected for each district in the November election. The fifth district would cover most of the western half of the state, from Kearney west. It would be larger in area than many states.

The next morning, early, Gaslin hitched his fine black Morgan mare to his ancient, one-seated buggy without a top, threw in his small trunk and cut across the prairie to Kearney where he could board the train to Plum Creek[*]. He did put on a fresh shirt and tie, and polished his old shoes.

He studied the buck board foot stools, slumped over in the

---

[*] Renamed Lexington

seat, and thought and thought. Did he, or did he not, want to get involved in the politics of a new statehood? There was always upheaval, often violent. Anyway, he was only one of several candidates at the convention, and could be defeated. Then, if nominated, he would have to run against a candidate on the Democratic side of the ballot. They would cut him to pieces. It was too scary to contemplate.

At the Plum Creek Hotel he met the man who would put his name in the pot. He also ran into C. J. Dilworth, an old friend and candidate for the judgeship. He had been a general in the Union Army. "I understand someone will nominate me," said Dilworth.

"The more the merrier," laughed Gaslin. "I sort of hope you get it. I'm not sure I want it."

Both names were put in the next day's caucus. There were some heated, but usually friendly debates. In the end Gaslin won. "Then I want C. J. as my district attorney," insisted Gaslin. Dilworth won that nomination without opposition.

"We'll be a great team. I'll need you," he told Dilworth, whom he would later call "very able, affable, and judicious, and one of the bravest and coolest of men."

They all celebrated with a beef dinner in the dining room and a few toasts. The banquet speaker warned them not to "underestimate the job if elected. You will earn your pay, I assure you."

"Maybe at the next convention we'll eat honest beef," said Gaslin to C. J. "Maybe butchers will be more prone to buy beef from ranchers than from cattle thieves, once we put the rustlers out of business."

Gaslin won easily and moved to Kearney. He expected court business to be brisk, but he little expected to preside over 69 murder trials in the next 16 years and sent many to the hangman's loop. As yet, this area was largely unsettled. Counties were laid out, but law and order were far from established. Lack of court facilities, if he found any, bothered him. He quickly learned they might be a small log, sod or frame building or no buildings at all. Officials worked around each other to take care of what county business there was, including court. As the homesteaders drove the cattlemen from the free range, there was bound to be friction. Large cattle companies hoped the settlers would pick the valleys and leave the rolling hills for them. But there was one problem: if grangers fenced their land, how would cattle get to water?

In the past, most crime never got to court. Little attention was paid to barroom brawls. Victims were buried in boot hill cemeteries without ceremony. If court was held, Judge Gaslin could expect it might be in a small room crowded with the criminal's friends, guns loaded and visible. Those charged previously often defied the judge and prosecuting attorney to convict. Cattle and horse thieves had stolen with impunity. This was what faced the judge of the new Nebraska Fifth Judicial District, and Gaslin didn't underestimate the challenge.

He purchased a home in Kearney near C. J. Dilworth long before he would take office in January. They met often to plan their circuit. They met in February for the first circuit, going to Holdrege, then Red Cloud and up the Republican Valley. Most of the cases were not particularly exciting, and quickly adjudicated, but their courage would soon be tested.

Their first tough case was a murder somewhere out there. (The location was not given for some reason.) The accused was a scroungy-looking character with tobacco juice running down his beard, maybe 50 years old. It was evident he had been there before, judging by the way his gun-toting friends crowded into the makeshift courtroom. The accused expected the usual – that is, bluffing the judge and going free.

Judge Gaslin and J. C. Dilworth came into the courtroom after the bailiff loudly announced his "Hear ye, Hear ye."

Gaslin opened his brief case, pulled out two huge pearl handled Colt revolvers, and laid them on the crude bench. C. J. did likewise. The judge announced, "We're here to hold a trial, and justice will be done."

The criminal and his cohorts noticeably wilted. When the short trial ended, after the jury announced the man guilty of murder in the first degree, Gaslin ordered him "hanged until dead."

This may have helped to establish his reputation as the "Hanging Judge." He soon sentenced so many to be hanged as, he took on the criminal element, that he quickly earned the title.

"Think we did all right," said Gaslin over supper that night.

"We sure did!" smiled Dilworth.

It would be several years before he was challenged again.

Gaslin found an appalling lack of court facilities as he worked his way around his circuit, although he was not surprised. Dilworth and he soon learned that found courthouses were mere hastily constructed shacks in which the county officials worked around each other. On Sunday there might be a church service in the same building. For court sessions the room, often about the size of a large living room, was converted into a courtroom. Jurors crammed into one corner, spectators in the back, the judge up front, and the accused and attorney in front of him. A cheap cast iron stove heated the building poorly and the judge often wore his horsehide coat in cold weather. If there were no courthouse built yet, court was held in the nearest building of sufficient size, even a saloon.

Gaslin held court when he arrived, and didn't quit until the case was settled, even if late at night. Smelly coal oil lamps lighted the room. The court reporter squinted and hoped his "scratchings" would be readable later. People crowded into the room until body odors became unbearable. On warm days, spectators sweated and bumped into each other, and cursed the conditions. But it was the most exciting thing to happen on the frontier, and who would dare miss it?

Gaslin under such conditions reverted easily to his sloppy dress habits - open shirt with no necktie. He wore a cheap pair of pants and, maybe, no socks. His hair was often uncombed and disheveled.

On the other hand Dilworth, tall and handsome with black hair and dark complexion of skin, like the true soldier, dressed with more dignity. He wore a dark suit, white shirt and black tie, and tried to keep them neatly pressed and clean. It was difficult, however arriving at the court after the long travel, dust and sweat. He tried, but he didn't succeed very well.

On December 5, 1876, in Buffalo County, Ira Nichols filed a warrant for the arrest of Albin C. Nash and William S. Nash (son) of said county for the theft on or about June 15, 1876, of five cows, value of $125, five steers, value of $175, one three-year-old steer, value of $35, three two-year-olds, value of $90, two yearling cattle, value of $40. Also included in the charge was cowboy W. Smith.

They were to be arrested in Buffalo County or wherever they could be found elsewhere in Nebraska.

Albin C. Nash came from Massachusetts to Michigan, then Illinois, then to Kearney in 1873. He had always been a hog and cattle dealer but in Kearney he established a butcher shop. He bought a number of cattle, however he used the purchased cattle as a front, making sure, apparently, that he would have enough allowing him to help himself to range cattle.

He was not alone; Buffalo County Sheriff Dave Anderson told Gaslin and Dilworth, "It would be unfair to charge Nash with all the cattle stealing during the past three years. The number of stolen cattle is simply enormous; from stealing the homesteader's yoke of oxen used for summer work, to the drover whose herds number in the thousands."

It was dangerous to leave cattle fit for market. With the land stretching far and wide, the chance of detection being small and the temptation great. Ranch owners seldom caught sight of their cattle except during spring and fall roundup. A few ranchers had some line riders who attempted to keep herds within certain fictional boundaries.

But Nichols kept better track of his cattle. He came from Pennsylvania and became a cattle dealer; keeping cattle in Lincoln and Dawson Counties. The cattle in question were from a herd that he purchased from Dent and Adams in July 1875. He branded with "M" on the left side or left hip. His cattle ran on the east of Ft. McPherson and on the north side of the Platte River. When the cattle came up missing he filed charges against Nash and his son. He had been suspicious of Nash for some time. Judge Gaslin set the trial for Sept. 1876.

CHAPTER FIVE

The "Olive Gang"

1876

District Attorney C. J. Dilworth and Judge William Gaslin sipped coffee in the office of Buffalo County Sheriff Dave Anderson in Kearney, discussing the crime situation in the sprawling Fifth Judicial District of Nebraska. This they often did in an effort to curb crime, especially cattle rustling. They knew it would not end until there was war of sorts between free-range cattle producers and the rapidly growing population of homesteaders. Most newcomers were honest law abiding men and women seeking free homes for themselves and their families. However, there were sure to be the not-so-law-abiding among them - those who made a business of rustling cattle, then selling them to the Indian agencies. Then they might steal them back from the Indians, thus creating more animosity. All of this on top of the murderous outlaws promised that Gaslin's court would be a busy court.

Right now the issue of stealing cattle from big cattle producers was the focus of these men. No one worried about the man who butchered a steer to feed his hungry family. That was acceptable for now. However, someday, somewhere in the Nebraska Fifth District, someone would hang or kill a small-time rustler and the range war would be on. This worried the men, and now Sheriff Anderson offered a new worry.

"I'm worried," said the sheriff. "Right now I'm concerned about these new neighbors in Custer County who are building headquarters near Custer City and new homes in Plum Creek." [*]

It surprised Dilworth that he didn't know about them. "Who could they be? Sounds as if they come with plenty of gold."

"It's the Olive brothers, Print, Ira and Bob. They trailed their cattle & horses from Texas. They're dropping them off some ten miles apart for 50 miles along the Middle Loup and South Loup Rivers from Dunning south and east as far as eastern Custer

---

[*] Renamed Lexington

County," said Anderson. "They may do fine, I hope so. However, the telegrams I am receiving from Texas don't make them look so good. Print has a hot temper and has killed men in Texas. So has Bob, who left with a price on his head. He has assumed the alias of Henry Stevens. I think lawmen in Texas are glad to be rid of them."

Gaslin, arranging his next schedule, perked up. "What else do you know about them?"

"Quite a bit, from several sheriffs. Mainly the brawls were over longhorn cattle the men roped and hassled from Texas grasslands. It seems a man named Maverick once owned many cattle, but the price before the Civil War was so low he didn't even bother to brand. The hills here are full of unbranded cattle appropriately named 'mavericks'."

According to the wires received by Anderson the Olive sons came home after the war and began roping and branding these cattle. They soon became wealthy, driving longhorn cattle along the famous Chisholm and Goodnight Trails to various shipping points in Kansas and even to Ogallala in Nebraska.

There was much competition. But there were also those who preferred rustling cattle gathered by someone else rather than do the hard work themselves.

The sheriffs of several Texas counties explained to Anderson how the Olives rode hard and had thousands of cattle to show for it. Soon there were arguments with neighbors over these "free" cattle and the Olives were involved in several shooting sprees. Print was tried for murder and acquitted. Their enemies, determined to wipe out the Olive Clan, attacked them one night at a branding corral. The Olives learned of it and prepared. However, the one assigned guard was asleep when the battle started. Thomas Olive was killed, and Print was wounded but survived.

Print, furious over the incident and this brazen action by outlaws who had most of the small cattlemen too frightened to resist, rode to his sheriff's office and tacked up a sign warning that "anyone caught with Olive-branded livestock will be shot on sight."

Deciding they'd had enough, Print, Ira and Bob rounded up 15,000 cattle and 4,000 horses, divided them into three herds, and headed north to Nebraska.

"I was told Bob is the more hot tempered of the brothers, and the one most often in trouble with the law and the neighbors," said

Anderson. "It didn't help any after one of the rustlers and a carpetbagger named Cal Nutt, met Bob in a saloon in 1876. He badgered Nutt into a gunfight. Nutt's shot missed and Bob shot him dead. He ducked the Texas Rangers and caught up with the herds when they were out of Texas. This is when he changed his name to Henry Stevens."

The Olives first found range in southwest Nebraska, but it was crowded and not to Print's liking. That same year a brother, Jay Olive, died as the result of a gunfight. Print went home for the funeral by train, but Bob dared not. That fall Print had Bob scout for better range. He found it along the Dismal River, and the along the South to the Middle Loup Rivers.

"What Print didn't consider was that the eastern edge of this range would be much too close to the western movement of homesteaders," said Dilworth, "Their fight over ownership of cattle may switch to fights with homesteaders over land."

"I can see trouble brewing as homesteaders settle in the middle of the Olive range," added Gaslin.

Gaslin was right about that, except this time it would be over a homesteader using the "long rope" (steeling cattle) and selling illegal meat, not ownership of land.

CHAPTER SIX

The Farmer and the Cowman Don't Mix

1877

Judge Gaslin and district attorney Dilworth, returning from a pleasant but uneventful Fifth District Court trip to Sidney 200 miles to the west end of the district, reminded each other that a cattle-stealing trial awaited them in Kearney.

Cases in Sidney and Ogallala ended in some convictions and a few acquittals. Then it was back for the trial of Nash and his two sons, charged with stealing cattle from the herds of Ira Nichols.

"Pretty nice to be able to ride the cushions of this passenger car," commented Dilworth. "Riding on the train sure beats riding your cheap buckboard behind old Dolly across the hills and staying at low class hotels in some remote place. Right, Judge?"

"This trial may give us some trouble," said Gaslin ignoring Dilworth's gibe at his stingy ways. "Many butchers buy stolen beef, risky as it is. Although most of it comes already butchered which takes care of the brand problem. With so many cattle around, it's quite a temptation to the unscrupulous. We can handle this one, but what if Print Olive finds hides carrying his brand dumped in some ravine?"

The two men left the train car and walked immediately to the Buffalo County courthouse. The sheriff and the county judges had the trial well organized. Ira Nichols was there as well as the Nashes and their attorneys. Nash didn't seem too worried.

Jury selection took some time. Local residents mostly farmers and ranchers, were reluctant to get involved in this case.

Finally a 12-man jury was in place. The bailiff called out the usual "Hear ye, Hear ye." This time the judge entered minus his Colts, which he left in his brief case. He even wore his robe and socks. He rapped the gavel.

Nichols was called first to testify.

"My home is in Pennsylvania. My business is raising and dealing in cattle. We keep our cattle in Lincoln and Dawson Counties. We purchased this herd (the herd from which the cattle were allegedly stolen) from Dent and Adams in July 1875. We don't sell cattle in the country except the maimed and then only directly to butchers. We brand with a "96" on the left side and left hip.

"Our principal ranch is about four miles below Ft. McPherson, and the lower ranch is 20 miles below that in Dawson County; some time early in October (1876), I learned that some of our cattle had been run off. I came down, and saw the Buffalo and Dawson County sheriffs in regard to it. That must have been about the 1st of November. After making investigations, I had Mr. Smith and the Three Nashes arrested."

George W. Smith called to the stand stated:
"I had been working for Nash part of the year at various things," said Smith. "Most of the time tending cattle that he kept at different places on the Loup (South Loup River north of Kearney) until some time in April and then we brought them and turned them in the Island." (Presumably in the Platte River).

"He (Nash) was engaged in the butcher business at that time. I had conversation with Nash in the spring in relation about going up there and getting cattle. He said he was running short of cattle to butcher and that he would have to have cattle and we were to go and get cattle. We were to get them here the best way we could.

"William S. Nash (son) was to go with me and so he got a horse and we started. A. C. Nash (another son) was to go to Plum Creek[*] to buy some cattle on the 'blind' and we were going to drive them back. We went up the south side of the Platte River and we did not see him. We got the cattle and drove them to a certain place south of Plum Creek. We were to hold them there the first night and during the next day to then proceed to drive them to Williamsburg. We were to hold them there until the next day and then drive them to the bridge and he would receive them, and we did so. It was understood that we were to cut cattle out of the Bent herd any time after dark that we could get them, and not let anyone see us…"

"I noticed the brand '96'. Alvin Nash (a son of Alvin C. Nash) and I took the cattle up the south side of the Platte." (Here Smith's testimony seems confused, sometimes sounding as if his

---

[*] Renamed Lexington

testimony involved another rustling job). "The first person we talked to was Cuttebeck who keeps a sheep ranch on the south side of the Platte... We also met an Englishman on the road and stopped to talk with him. We watered our horses there. We came back with the cattle part of the time the same way as we went up. It was about nine o'clock in the morning after we got back..."

"Nash told us he would like to have a bill of sale, and I went into the house and wrote one and signed it 'T. M. Williamson', a fictitious name. I understood he was to go to and see Leffling at Plum Creek about buying some cattle as a 'blind'."

In cross-examination Nash's attorney accused the prosecution of making a promise or hint that the case against Smith would be dropped if he turned state's evidence.

Smith had been arrested at Ogallala on December 3, 1876. Nash said he had a few words with Smith before he quit working for him.

Albin Nash's testimony was long, but he indicated denial of all of Smith's testimony. He had bought some "96" but had them branded and turned into his corrals.

The prosecution examined George Bleakman. He said, "I live in Phelps County on the south side of the Platte, 14 miles west of the bridge. The men stopped at my well to water their horses. Later I saw Nash and Smith go back with cattle. I watched them through my field glasses."

The jury after some deliberation voted Alvin C. Nash guilty of cattle stealing.

Judge Gaslin leaned back in his chair, quietly considering the jury's verdict. He paused some time, and then spoke deliberately:

"We have been told by Sheriff Anderson that you're not the only cattle rustler around, that it is going on all over the country even to stealing a farmer's oxen or a poor family's milk cow. This has to stop. You may not always steal the cattle, but I suspect that sometimes you knowingly buy stolen cattle and sell the meat in your market. I sentence you to seven years in the Nebraska penitentiary."

William Gaslin and district attorney Dilworth sat in the train depot in Kearney waiting to board, to adjudicate cases in Sidney and counties in between. He brought along the latest issue of the

Kearney New Era newspaper. Local editors carried not only stories of local crime but also stories of crime from distant newspapers. It filled up space and increased readership. These stories often revealed the course of crime in the judge's wide-ranging district. This morning's paper was especially interesting. He handed it to Dilworth.

"Read this. We might have our first train robbers in court. They robbed a train west of here."

Dilworth wasn't impressed with the prospect. "They're probably a hundred miles away by this time. Who's to stop them? It would take the army in Sidney a day or so just to get ready to chase them. They won't live off the land and travel light as the robbers."

He took the paper and read the article after boarding; it was copied from the Daily Press in Sidney:

Big Springs, a lonely station on the Union Pacific seventy miles west of North Platte, was the scene of a bold, successful train robbery last night. Passenger train No. 4 was due at Big Springs at 10:40 p.m. Patterson, conductor, and George Vorman, engineer, were bringing the train to a halt. The station agent, who was sitting at his desk waiting for it, was startled by the appearance of two men with drawn revolvers, who ordered him to throw up his hands. They, being two to one and he unarmed. He was compelled to comply.

They then proceeded to tear out the telegraph instruments, which they carried off and threw away. They hung out the red lantern, which was a signal for the train to stop for orders. As soon as the train stopped it was taken possession of by a number of masked men, variously estimated from two to twenty, who made their appearance. All were heavily armed with revolvers and repeating rifles. Four of them went to the engine and ordered the engineer and fireman to throw up their hands. The engineer stepped down on the other side of the engine and they sent bullets after him. All of them obeyed orders to throw up their hands...

The article continued to describe the robbery in great detail, how the robbers tried to force the "express messenger" to open the safe. He insisted he didn't have the combination, and the men beat him over the head with their guns, inflicting severe wounds. Finally, they decided he really didn't have the combination. The safe contained $50,000 in gold. They broke open three coin boxes containing $60,000 in cash. They robbed passengers of gold watches and cash.

The station agent and others knew that several men were camping in the bluffs north of Big Springs. Later, it was surmised the leader was Sam Bass who had come through earlier with a herd of cattle headed for the Black Hills. It was also learned that Bass gambled away the cattle money and had no money with which to repay the Texas rancher who trusted him with his herd.

The editor of this newspaper also quoted more from the Daily Press. "Now that the horse is stolen they will likely proceed to lock the door."

"Pretty exciting," offered Dilworth. "If we hear from him again he'll be in Texas. We might get him back for trial, but I doubt it. I predict he won't resist such easy money and won't quit until the Texas Rangers take care of him."

The conductor came back to visit with the judge and district attorney. "I see you're reading all about the train robbery," he said. "Our detectives are following Bass. We'll get him sooner or later, as we think he will continue robbing trains in Texas. I'll keep you informed. He needed this money badly to pay for the cattle he sold in the Black Hills and proceeded to lose to gambling."

This case never came before Judge Gaslin, as Bass got away from Nebraska and died in a gun battle with the Texas rangers after he robbed trains there.

Meanwhile the Olives, with herds strung from the Dismal River all the way to Clear Creek in Custer County, moved their cows to the lower end of the ranch to calve under the protection of the hills and trees. All over their range the grass was tall, rich and sure to put extra pounds on the steers. Their ranch buildings were large with huge corrals of native logs. Their homes in Lexington were lavish. No one could claim a better range setup.

The Mitchell-Ketchum wagons on their journey from St. Paul drove southwest after their stop at Loup City picked a spot to settle. It was on a rise a half-mile north of Clear Creek, where they filed on adjoining quarter sections and set to work building a sod house on the line between the properties. While Mitchell finished the house, Ketchum plowed 20 acres of native sod and planted corn. That is, he cut holes in the overturned sod and dropped in kernels of corn. The crop came up quickly in the rich earth.

When Sheriff Anderson picked up new homestead filings he was shocked to read of the Mitchell-Ketchum filing in the midst of Print's favorite cow and calving range.

He relayed the news to Gaslin and Dilworth at their next meeting. "This will mean trouble. Homesteaders usually settle near the edge of settlements and they're hard to stop. But to settle in the middle of Olive's favorite calving range took a lot of courage, or is plain dumb."

Judge Gaslin studied his shoes for a time. "I know the men are right but there needs to be some common sense in all this."

The Judge's worry was not about homes in Olive territory, but about skinning other people's cattle and selling the meat to area butchers.

During spring roundup when branding calves, Print noticed the new homesteader north of Clear Creek and he also noticed a man tending a patch of corn. Bob, Print's brother (alias Henry Stevens) grumbled about plowing up good grass.

"Do you suppose we could work out a deal with the settlers where they could have the bottom land and leave the hills for cattle?" mused Print as they looked over several cows calving and others with small calves warming in the sun.

"They would fence their land and then where would our cattle get water?" replied Bob.

The next spring Ketchum, encouraged by the previous year's yield of corn, planted the same acres and added a few more. Then he drove to Kearney and brought home several rolls of barbwire. He cut ash and cedar posts in the hills and soon had his cornfield fenced with four strands of barbwire, stretched tight.

"I'd like to see the long horn cow that can get through that fence unless she has help," Ami remarked to Mitchell that night at supper.

The rains came in time, and in August Ami's corn stood shoulder high. "I'm sure it will make 40 bushels per acre," he boasted.

Ami was also a blacksmith. One day two Print cowboys rode by and asked him to shoe their mounts for winter riding. When finished, they rode around the cornfield toward one of Olive's line camps.

The next morning Mitchell looked out his door on the west side of the cabin. There, a herd of longhorns munched away at the tender, tasty corn stalks. The field already looked as if a tornado had swept through it. Mitchell called Ami to look. He cursed for five minutes and then went out to investigate the other side of the field.

"Those bastards cut the wires right down the middle on the west side," Ami told Mitchell, "Hell, two can play at this game."

"What do you mean?" asked Mitchell, alarmed and suspicious.

"You'll see!"

The next morning Ketchum came in with a wagon load of beef carcasses.

Where did you get that?" asked Mitchell.

"I told you two could play at this game."

"You're asking for a wagon load of trouble," cautioned the horrified Mitchell. "The Olives will kill you for this or hang you under the nearest cottonwood. They're madder than hornets now over people butchering beef and selling it in town. And you know how hot headed Stevens is."

"I can take care of myself. I can shoot as well as they", said Ami.

Mitchell was angry as well as frightened. "You're in this by yourself. I don't want anything to do with it."

Meantime Judge Gaslin learned that Harrington (alias Doc Middleton), the quiet cowboy who shot his way out of a fight in a Sidney saloon[***], had set up headquarters in Robber's Roost, a deep canyon northeast of Olive headquarters in Custer county. Print didn't like the idea, nor did Gaslin. Two hombres in one place would be a threat to peace.

"Middleton appears to have graduated to horse stealing in a big way," said Dilworth "Could be trouble there as well. Stevens warned Middleton not to mess with the Olive horses."

However, Middleton assured the Olives he wouldn't touch their horses. Doc was seeking a good hideout since cattlemen west of here are offering big rewards for his capture, dead or alive.

[***] See story about Harrington on top of page 24

****

Sometimes Gaslin drove by Mrs. Harrolson's farm south of Kearney, watching her tend her crops aided by three small children, all under ten. Her husband had died just as he was about to "prove up" on the homestead.

"That's tough," he told Anderson the next time they met in Kearney, "But give her credit for trying very hard to carry on. I asked one day if she needed help but she assured me she didn't."

Then one day a tall suave gentleman, well dressed, stopped in for a drink of water. He chatted a while, patting the children on their heads. She confided that she was about to "prove up" on her homestead but was not sure how to do it.

"I'm not too busy," said the man giving his name as S. D. Richards. "I'll stick around and help."

However, the more Richards stuck around the more suspicious she became. She felt he was giving her bad advice and was afraid he was planning to gyp her out of her farm. It was common for men to look for what became known as "Widow Claim Hunting", that is "quick riches" by wooing a recent widow whose husband had suffered a bad demise.

She confided in a neighbor, who told her to get rid of the man. One day she said to Richards, "I don't need your services any longer."

A few days later this same neighbor, noting a lack of activity around the farm, stopped to investigate. He found the family slain in a most gruesome manner. He rode to Kearney to report to the sheriff. "I think it was this man Richards," he said, "I saw him there several times." Neighbors and citizens of Kearney were outraged, threatening the hanging of Richards if ever caught.

Sheriff Anderson checked out train traffic and decided Richards had fled east. He called the Pinkerton Detective Agency. He rode a train to Chicago and met with a Pinkerton agent. They searched out many leads but which led nowhere. The men researched certain leads in other towns.

In Steubenville, Ohio, Anderson and the agent found a man who resembled Richards. They arrested him, questioned him, and decided he should be charged with the murder. Anderson took him by train to Nebraska.

It was common practice, when necessary, for passengers to

ride the caboose of a freight train. This is what Anderson did when he left Omaha and came west with Richards.

At Grand Island a telegram was waiting from Sheriff Anderson's wife, Maggie. "Large mob at Kearney Depot. Stop. Ready with rope on pole, stop, planning to overpower you, stop."

Anderson wired her right back. "Meet me at Buda (a small way station five miles east of Kearney.) Hitch up the fastest team we have."

Maggie slipped away from the jail stables with team and buggy and drove the five miles to Buda by a round about way to slip away from the mob waiting outside the jail, letting them think she was off to the post office and to avoid any informers along the way. In the days before much cultivation the prairie was flat and easy to drive over.

The exceptions were dried buffalo wallows, where buffalo fought flies and wallowed in the mud after heavy rains. In dry weather these dried rock solid. If a buggy were to hit a wallow at full speed it could fly in the air and easily overturn.

Maggie reached the Buda station before the train. When it stopped at Buda the sheriff put Richards in the buggy on Maggie's left, his feet shackled to the iron foot rests and his manacled hands fastened securely to the arm of the buggy seat to prevent him from interfering in any way with her driving,

The conductor yelled at the train crew to hurry and unload the small amount of freight they had for Buda and then he shouted at the engineer and fireman "to get up steam for a quick trip to Kearney," as he wanted to beat Maggie to the jail.

Trainmen told the Buda telegraph agent to notify the Kearney depot that Sheriff Anderson's wife had taken Richards off the train and that he was being taken to jail by Maggie as fast as her team could take them.

"I warn you," Anderson threatened the operator, "if you wire word of Richards' removal I will arrest you on the spot, put you in the buggy with Richards and have Maggie put you in jail when she gets there. Maggie, use the buggy whip on the horses and don't slow down on your trip to the jail for any reason."

Maggie did use the whip, and the buggy and its passenger left the station in a whirl of dust as she raced ahead of the engine. The train soon caught up with her but she followed along side for three and one-half miles. Then she swung south to the jail located about one half mile south of the depot. The engineer whistled constantly hoping the horses would run away and upset the buggy. He had good reason to hope the team might run away and upset the buggy when she hit the buffalo wallows, as he wanted Richards hung after he heard the story of the widow and her poor children.

There was no trail so Maggie took the shortest way and hit the buffalo wallows at breakneck speed. The buggy catapulted in the air crazily with many a near upset. Richards was beside himself with fright, screaming and cursing at the top of his voice.

"Maggie, I would rather be hung than dragged to death in manacles," he screamed. "I could kill you far more mercifully than the way you're gonna kill both of us. Just take me to the jail slow-like and let me be hung by that mob."

By the time, the freight train reached the station Maggie was still a mile and a half from the depot. Fortunately, the engineer was so intent on beating Maggie to the depot to warn the lynchers that he failed to slow enough to stop at the depot and slid past a quarter of a mile. By the time he backed to the depot Maggie was headed for the jail.

Maggie swung southwest. Her horses were fagged but she whipped them all the more until she reached the jail, their sides heaving and frothing with sweat. The whole ride took only 20 minutes, a record in itself. The deputies rushed Richards into the jail, into an inner cell and locked the doors with the heaviest padlocks.

Richards turned to the deputies and said. "I'm sure glad to see this jail. If I had my druthers I would rather take my chances with the mob than take a buggy ride with Maggie."

When Anderson stepped off the train without Richards the mob set up a racket.

"Where's Richards?"

"He's in jail where he should be. My wife just drove him there."

The gang rushed to the jail, ropes in hand, but the deputies held them off with shotguns.

The other prisoners hated Richards so much the sheriff had to keep him in a separate cell and would not allow him into the corridor for fear the other men would kill him.

When Anderson was through reciting the tale of Maggie's buggy ride, Judge Gaslin was laughing so hard he could scarcely discuss what to do with the prisoner.

"The crime was committed in Kearney County so the trial would have be held there," explained Gaslin. "Take Richards to Lincoln for safekeeping until I can set the trial date."

Late that night Anderson and Richards boarded a train to Lincoln.

If horse thieves were doing well in the Fifth Judicial District, cattle rustlers were doing even better, much to the frustration of Judge Gaslin and District Attorney Dilworth.

"Remember what we said about eating honest beef?" said Gaslin. "We'll have to put that off a while if all the stories floating around on the frontier telegraph are true."

"We don't seem to be reducing this crime much."

"Ketchum is more brazen than ever," noted Anderson when they met at his office to discuss the cattle-stealing situation. "And he seems to be getting support from your cohort Judge Aaron Wall of Loup City in Sherman County. When they deliver the meat to a butcher shop they call it, slow elk. But we know there are no elk in Custer County. They feel safe. The Olives suspect them and others, but what can they do? Once the hide is off there is no proof of ownership since carcasses carry no brands.

"Olives can hear the cows bawl and know the calves have been taken. Bob Olive has found hides in the creeks and draws, some from two and three-year-old steers."

Anderson told of a trial held in Sweetwater, a small village on the north edge of Buffalo County near the Sherman County line.

The Olives didn't have much proof, but they were suspicious of Judge Wall and his client. Wall had a homestead in Buffalo County below the county line where he was suspected of stashing the carcasses in a cave until he could deliver them to customers.

Custer County Judge E. C. Boblits conducted the trial. Wall's client, another nearby homesteader, was accused of stealing Olive cattle. Olives brought their attorney from Plum Creek.[*] Wall argued that the trial couldn't be held in Buffalo County since the cattle were stolen elsewhere. The courtroom was in the middle of the room of

---

[*] Current day Lexington

the village's only business, a grocery store and post office.

When Wail saw he was losing the case, he shamelessly took his client from the courtroom and fled on horseback.

The surprised Judge Boblits was slow to determine what happened. Meanwhile, Wall and the rustler were gaining more space between them all the time. He suddenly realized they were headed for Loup City in Sherman County.

Boblits quickly gathered a posse, which included Print and Bob Olive. When they tried to arrest the men on Loup City's Main Street the crafty Wall invited them to come into the Massassoit House (hotel) "for a more comfortable place to discuss the matter." They didn't know the new courthouse had burned and this hotel was their temporary courthouse. When they entered the dining room and gathered around the dining room table the judge rapped his gavel and called court to order. The bewildered and angry Judge Boblits and the posse felt they didn't dare touch him, and rode out of town,

Judge Gaslin laughed. "You have to hand it to that crafty judge, but he'll be lucky if he lives long. He'd be smart to try some honest hard work if half the stories we hear about the Olives are true."

The three men later heard more stories about Judge Wall and his problems with the Olives. Print and Bob were not about to let him get away from their long rope and the nearest cottonwood tree. However, they had to catch him away from Loup City and the courthouse.

Another time, the Olives cornered Wall on the main street in Loup City. Print whirled his lariat loop prepared to lay it over Judge Wall's neck when a Sherman County cattleman by the name of Fletcher, whose reputation matched the Olives, rode up and said, "Throw that loop and you're a dead man." Since he had a gun in his hand rather than a rope, Print let the rope slowly fall to the ground, whirled around and rode out of town, his men following.

"I can understand the Olive's frustration and anger in all of this," said Judge Gaslin when told the story, "But we can't have people taking the law into their own hands."

"You have to smile a little when this crafty Judge Wall can outwit the Olives," answered Dilworth as they drove down the road to another trial. "They could have shot him as they are more used to doing, but I think they thought hanging would a better warning to the rustlers. I'm sure now we will have a terrible blowup before all this is settled between dishonest new comers and the cattlemen."

There were no doubts that early settlers, short on food and financial resources, butchered beef now and then. Sometimes this was ignored by cattlemen even to the point of taking a quarter of beef to a hungry family. But to intentionally sell the beef to a butcher shop was another matter.

"I can understand people's frustration with the law because of the way trials are so often handled," continued Gaslin as they passed another new sod home being built along the way. "I can understand their frustration with the Nebraska Supreme Court turning criminals lose after they have spent scarce dollars on trials. However, this mob rule is ruining our court system. We must abide by the law and not take it into our own hands. Innocent people will be hung this way, and some may be denied a fair trial."

Gaslin was thinking of Smith, who murdered Collins on his Buffalo County farm and was sent to prison for life. "The damn Supreme Court sent him back for a new trial," he said, "It cost Buffalo County $15,000 and the people were furious. If they had it to do over, they'd let it be known, they would hang him before the trial. Just as they would do to Richards now if they had the chance."

Judge Gaslin was given a special assignment to conduct a trial over a horrible murder in Nebraska City. It appears two black men, Martin and Jackson, having completed terms in the state prison, were released. They came to Nebraska City where they attacked 60-year-old Charles Slocum, murdered him and "outraged" (raped) his wife. They were brought to trial under Gaslin. It was a short trial; the jury awarded a verdict of murder in the second degree. The judge sentenced them to life in prison, as was his policy for murder in the second degree.

The whole trial so incensed the local citizenry that they took the law into their own hands. That night they overpowered the jailer, broke down the jail door and unlocked the iron cage where the prisoners were confined. They took them a few blocks south of the courthouse and found a suitable tree. They did allow the men to say their prayers. While Martin was saying his prayer Jackson laughed at him. "Both men died proclaiming their innocence," said a local news reporter.

"Anyway," said Gaslin, "the Supreme Court can't overturn that verdict."

On his way home he stopped in Lincoln at the state prison to visit his friend Warden Nobes. Nobes managed many of the criminals Gaslin was sending to his care. When they were comfortable in his office, he asked:

"Want to hear about a couple of young law-abiding citizens, one a son of Warden Dawson, who captured a prison escapee? It seems this man, Peter Wesselgartner, a horse thief, escaped from the penitentiary and these two boys captured him last May."

He showed the judge the newspaper account of their exploit:

> "Peter Wesselgartner, the horse thief who escaped from the penitentiary evening before last, was captured about ten o'clock yesterday morning at a farm house about ten miles east of Lincoln by the sixteen-year-old son of Warden Dawson and a young farm hand by the name of Charles Burt. Young Dawson and Burt started on horseback eastward after Wesselgartner immediately after supper, going east from the penitentiary. They learned that on the Baily farm three miles east of the city, the man partook of a hearty supper and then proceeded on east. A few miles farther on, he got off a wagon close to a house and left the road, going across the country through plowed fields. Here the boys took the trail and followed it perhaps a mile. They came to a farmhouse and distinctly heard voices of several men inside. After securing their horses, young Dawson walked to the front door while his companion stood guard at the back door.
>
> Dawson knocked and when the man of the house opened the door he inquired if there was a stranger in the house. The man replied "no." Dawson remarked that it was "too thin," bolted into the house and found his man seated at a table playing Seven Up. The moment Dawson entered Wesselgartner rose and made his way to the back door. Here Burt confronted him with a drawn revolver, who demanded his surrender. He paid no attention to the demand and fast left the house whereupon the boys shouted for him to stop or they would put a hole through him. He stopped suddenly and allowed the boys to pinion his arms to his back with a halter strap. In his plight he was compelled to walk four miles,

the boys riding behind him with drawn revolvers that contained a single load. At the end of four miles Wesselgartner refused to walk farther and laid down on the road.

Fortunately, a farmhouse was close. By loudly howling, the farmer was aroused and came to the rescue. His horses and wagon were pressed into service and the convict taken back to prison, arriving about 3:30 a.m."

"When I took charge of the man, "Nobes told Gaslin, "Just as I was about to open the cell door, he threw a handful of cayenne pepper in my eyes. However, a night guard brought down his nightstick on him, which brought him to time. He was carrying a large pocketknife with a ground down large blade, and other articles he had picked up while he was loose.

"He's one of the most dangerous characters in our prison. I told the boys never try that again."

CHAPTER SEVEN

Early Frontier Justice

1878

Bob Olive, alias Stevens, sat near the window of the coach as the passenger train pulled into Kearney and slowly rolled past the stock yards. He watched absentmindedly, just glad to be home and anxious to get to the ranch and cattle on the South and Middle Loup Rivers.

He was returning from a trip home to Texas to visit his aging parents, Mr. and Mrs. James Olive, and his wife. He tried to convince his wife to move to Nebraska. She wasn't convinced and he didn't stay long---the law still wanted him for murder. Posters in Texas post offices still offered a reward for him "dead or alive," His wife said, "Let's see if you can stay out of trouble up there first."

It was not as pleasant a trip as he had hoped, and so he was anxious to see the cattle, breathe fresh Nebraska air and visit a few cowboys. He suddenly perked up when he noticed cattle in the stockyards and wondered who was shipping cattle this late in the year. Olive steers and aging cows had already been shipped, which was why he had time for this trip home. He would take a look as soon as he got off the train.

Bob, walking over to the cattle, was shocked to note the cattle carried Print's brand. He knew Print, like so many cattlemen, didn't sell cattle locally. If he had sold to local buyers he would have cattle in the neighborhood with his brand. It was a wide-open invitation for the dishonest to add to their number "with the long rope and a hot iron." Too many Olive cattle were stolen as it was.

He walked down Main Street and stopped at the first meat market. "What do you know about the Olive cattle in the yards?"

"Sure. They're my cattle. I have a bill of sale for them."

"May I see it?" Bob studied the bill of sale for some time before handing it back. "That's a false bill of sale. 'Print Olive' signed this. He always signs his name I. P. Olive. Where did you get it?"

The butcher's face turned ashen. He hesitated. "I bought

them from Ketchum. I supposed he had purchased them from Print."

Bob immediately walked over to the sheriff's office. "He's been caught red handed, stealing our cattle. I think it is up to you to arrest Ketchum,"

It was plain to Bob that Sheriff Anderson was reluctant. "I would have to go into an organized county and try to arrest Ketchum, and he's noted as a crack shot with a rifle."

"How about deputizing me?"

"I can do that so long as you promise to bring him in alive and don't harm him first," said the sheriff.

"I can promise that but I'll have to take my own men with me. I wouldn't dare go up there alone."

Upon learning that Judge Gaslin and the district attorney were back in town from a long circuit, Anderson walked over to the their office. The more he thought about what he had done, the more nervous he became.

"We're sorry you did that, Dave," said Gaslin. "You know the Olive reputation for dealing with rustlers, not that Ketchum doesn't deserve some of it. But we have to stay within the law. I can see trouble brewing. Ketchum has been under Olive's suspicion for a long time.

"I already have an overload of 26 murder cases, most of them as unnecessary as this one may turned out to be."

Gaslin sent messages to both Print and Ketchum. "Print, why not pay Ketchum for the corn field destroyed by your cattle." And to Ketchum, "Why not pay for the stolen cattle?"

The suggestion went unheeded by both men.

November, 1878, Bob Olive alias Henry Stevens, cowboys Barney Armstrong, Pete Beaton and a settler named James McIndeffer saddled up horses that morning and rode to the Mitchell and Ketchum homesteads with Bob leading an extra horse. The purpose: to arrest Ketchum and take him to Kearney to be charged with stealing Olive cattle.

As the men rode up they could see Ketchum seated on a wagon with a bull tied to the rear of the box. Mitchell was standing at the east end of the house, rifle in hand. Ketchum had a revolver holstered at his right hip. Ketchum, a blacksmith, at first may have thought as he stepped down from the wagon seat that they wanted horses shod, which happens often this time of the year. However, as he noted their uncivil determination, he decided they had something else in mind. He placed his right hand on the revolver's butt.

Bob ignored Mitchell and rode directly to Ketchum.

"I have a warrant for your arrest from Sheriff Anderson, Ami," yelled Olive.

Ketchum made no response, so Bob repeated it, but this time quite close to the wagon, and the three men directly behind.

Instead, Ketchum drew his revolver and began firing and Olive returned the fire. Olive's horse, green broke, jumped away, bucked and became unmanageable. Both men missed, but continued to fire. Hit in the arm, Ketchum's left arm fell limp.

Olive looked back just in time to see Mitchell fire from a double-barreled needle gun[***], missing him narrowly.

"For God's sake, old man, don't shoot," shouted Olive. Mitchell's wife handed him another rifle. Olive lunged forward in the saddle just as Mitchell aimed carefully and fired. The bullet struck Olive in the lower back, lodging in his upper lungs and not far from his heart.

Olive clung to the saddle horn and rode away, blood gushing from the deadly wound. Armstrong and Beaton rode in to support Olive on either side of his horse. They raced down the slope. Ketchum and Mitchell kept on firing when two of Ketchum's bullets struck Beaton through the coat, barely missing his body, and hit Armstrong in the foot.

The Olive men, one on each side, assisted Bob as best they could in the saddle to Harrington's homestead some 90 rods down near the creek. They helped Olive to bed, still bleeding badly.

"I'm done for, boys," choked out Bob Olive as he lie back on the bed, still bleeding badly. McIndeffer and Armstrong rode hard to Kearney, got fresh horses and brought back Dr. C. T. Dildine, physician and surgeon late that night along with Sheriff Anderson. Dr. Dildine, after a quick inspection of the wound, said, "It's serious. The slug passed through his kidney and lodged in his lungs near his heart."

[***] A form of a muzzleloader, but with a needle that holds the bullet in position for greater accuracy.

The doctor gave Olive medications and offered little hope for his survival.

The next day Print and Ira arrived. Speaking now barely above a whisper, Bob Olive asked for a pencil and paper to make out his will. He left his property to his wife, still in Texas, and dispensed his personal items, saddles, chaps, guns and so forth to several friends, especially to Armstrong and Beaton who risked their lives to save him in the get away. "I want to be buried in Texas," were his last words.

Mitchell and Ketchum hurriedly threw a few items into the wagon and returned the borrowed bull to Dowse, then drove to Loup City to see Judge Aaron Wall. Ketchum sought a doctor to set his broken left arm.

"We want to drive to Custer City and turn ourselves in," said Mitchell.

"Don't do that," warned Wall. "Print will hang you for sure if you go there."

They decided to return to Merrick County from whence they came.

An inquest over the body of Bob Olive was held December I, 1878 in Kearney before Coroner F. I. Switz. Gaslin and Dilworth joined as observers. Armstrong, Beaton and Dr. Dildine were called as witnesses.

Armstrong was called first:

".... I am 23, work for Olive, taking care of cattle. Wednesday morning, Nov. 26, 1878, me and these two fellers went to arrest Ami Ketchum. Olive went past Mitchell, as we had nothing to do with him. The sheriff (meaning Olive as a deputized) told Ketchum to throw up his hands, told him a second time. He didn't throw them up but drew his six-shooter and commenced firing.

"Mitchell was off about 15 or 20 steps and, as Bob turned, Mitchell fired at him and shot him through the back. Bob said, "Don't shoot, old man,· but the old man fired on him anyway."

Q. Did Stevens fire the first shot?
A. No, Sir.
Q. How long did Stevens live after being shot?
A. Until half past three, Saturday.

Q. Where hit?
A. Just below the short rib in the back. The ball lodged in him; it was a long ball.

Switz next called H. Beaton.

"I am 21. Ketchum was about to start for Loup City. Bob rode up to Ketchum and told him to throw up his hands as he had papers for him."

Q. What was he going to arrest him for?
A. For stealing cattle, I believe.
Q. Did they keep on shooting?
A. Yes.
O. Was anyone else shot?
A. Ketchum shot me through the collar of my coat in two places. The old man shot through me the first shot fired. I think Mitchell is about 65. The rifle was a double-barreled rifle. Then the woman in the house ran out with a gun and handed it to Mitchell. He shot Bob with the second shot.

Dr. C. T. Dildine, 26, was called next.

He stated the ball passed through Olive's liver and lower lobes in the right lung.

Sheriff Anderson, 38, was called.

He stated:

"There was a warrant issued here by Justice Cannon, sworn out by the deceased, Henry Stevens (AKA Bob Olive), and handed to me and I deputized Stevens to make the arrest. I issued it November 19, 1878. He told me he went there to make the arrest and he saw Ketchum to the north of the house and the old man standing to the east. He passed by him and went to Ketchum and told him he had a warrant for him, and seeing the pistol, he told him to throw up his hands. Just at that instant he heard a shot and he saw Ketchum draw his pistol and he commenced firing at Ketchum. Getting his mount under control to some extent, he turned around and saw Mitchell had a gun leveled at him. He said 'for god's sake, old man, don't shoot.' He threw himself forward in the saddle and just at that instance he felt the shot in his side. The horse he brought for Ketchum to ride had disappeared as he high-tailed for home."

The proceedings of the inquest were filed Jan. 7, 1879 with

Frank Young, county clerk.

James Olive, Bob's father, came from Texas to claim the body and take it home for burial. Print swore revenge. That could only bring more troubles.

The area lawmen were most anxious to locate the fugitives before the Olives found them, as they knew that the Olives would not be just in their delivery of the law. Thus, November, 1878.... Mitchell and Ketchum were located and arrested by Merrick County Sheriff, William Letcher and taken to the jail In Kearney. Judge Gaslin decreed that the trial be held in Custer City (near present day Callaway), the county seat. Sheriff Anderson appointed Keith County Sheriff Barney Gillan to take prisoners Mitchell and Ketchum to Custer County for trial.

At his office in Kearney Judge Gaslin checked his schedule to determine when he could hold the trial in Custer City. District Attorney Dilworth worked on papers preparing for it. Gaslin and he discussed the problems of holding a trial in the little log cabin that passed as Custer County Court House.

"It is hardly a courthouse, it's Judge Boblits two-room ranch home. How could the jury, attorneys and witnesses be accommodated in so little space, let alone the huge crowd of spectators it will attract? I wonder if it could be held in Olive's big horse barn," mused Gaslin.

The barn was huge with doors on the north side and south side, both high enough that a person could ride in without dismounting. And, if he was in a hurry such as he might be if pursued, he could ride right on through and disappear in the rugged canyons to the north. There would be many ranchers at the trial, said Dilworth. Most of them had lost cattle to rustlers, not necessarily Ketchum or his sidekick Judge Aaron Wall. Beef was showing up all over the country in small town butcher shops. They knew legitimate beef was sold as two- to four-year-old steers and cull cows.... Some of the beef sold in the shops was from young animals, even calves, the kind ranchers never sold. Ketchum appeared to be a sort of ringleader, and so if the court convicted him maybe the traffic would slow down at least.

"We have no good place to hold a trial," added Dilworth. "No matter where it is held, ranchers with no sympathy for Ketchum will be there with guns strapped on. Getting a fair trial will be difficult."

December 9, 1878, Barney Gillan and prisoners Luther Mitchell and Ami Ketchum, wrists tied together, boarded the train in Kearney and stopped at Plum Creek.[*]

C. W. McNamar, attorney for Mitchell and Ketchum, also boarded a passenger train for Plum Creek. His gut feeling was that his clients were in great danger and would in no way get a fair trial. Maybe no trial at all if he knew anything at all about Print's temper and his tendency to draw a gun and ask questions later. From Plum Creek, Gillan and Philip Dufran, who accompanied him, were to take the accused men by spring wagon north 40 miles to the Olive Ranch where Judge Boblits was to meet them and hold the preliminary hearing. Mitchell would be accused of killing Bob Olive and both men for stealing cattle.

McNamar wanted to ride in the buggy and protect his clients but was told there was no room (there is room for three men in the back seat of a buggy). "Besides, you're not invited," said Dufran. Now McNamar's suspicions were confirmed; the two men were in serious danger. Also, why leave so late in the afternoon when normally they would have left early morning.

And so, at the livery stable, McNamar rented a team buckboard saying he wanted "a team that could travel fast and for a long distance."

"This is the best I have, but remember Gillan also has the best team Print Olive has."

"When Gillan leaves I want to be on his tail," added McNamar, "I don't trust him and Dufran."

---

[*] Renamed Lexington

The Old Olive Ranch. Cowboys preparing to intercept the Officers who are bringing Mitchell and Ketchum into Custer County for trial. Re-enacted by S.D. Butcher, photographer and provided by the Nebraska State Historical Society Photograph Collections.

When Gillan, Dufran and the prisoners left late that afternoon and headed north on the well-traveled trail, McNamar pulled in right behind them. When Gillan looked back he appeared surprised. He whipped his team into a fast trot. McNamar did likewise. Days were short this time of year, and 20 miles out he was having trouble keeping them in sight as dusk settled over the hills. When it became dark he lost them entirely. The moon came up but it was hidden behind clouds most of the time. He didn't dare push his team harder or they would be played out before reaching Custer City.

McNamar stopped at the Able Ranch to water his team and let them rest a few minutes. Gillan had done likewise but for a very brief stop. It was obvious he didn't intend for McNamar to get too close.

Around midnight McNamar noticed the horses perk up their ears and look right. There in the darkness, he could make out figures on horseback. At first he thought of Indians. Then the moon broke through and he could make out the features of Print Olive and two men behind him riding at a high canter. They soon disappeared in the darkness. Now he was nervous. He pushed his team harder, but they were tiring.

He negotiated Devil's Gap, a steep incline south of the South Loup River. He heard a loud boom. He could smell prairie grass on fire and gunpowder. Now, he was even more apprehensive. He hurried to Custer City and there he awakened Judge Boblits.
"Have you seen Gillan and the prisoners?" McNamar asked. "Not a thing. They were supposed to have been brought to the Olive Ranch for the hearing but when they didn't show, I came home. Come in and stay the night. We'll look for them in the morning."

The previous afternoon Print Olive, accompanied by Bill Green, owner of the Wild West Saloon, and Jack Baldwin, hotel owner, left his home in Plum Creek[*] on three of Olive's best horses, horses that could travel 50 miles and hardly take a deep breath. The men were well fortified by frequent drags from Green's whiskey jug. They passed McNamar far enough to the side that Olive hoped he wouldn't recognize him. "That damn moon," he mumbled to the men.

Olive and the men caught up with Gillan below Devil's Gap and rode to the Olive Ranch where they imbibed more liquor. Print needed to be well fortified to give him the courage to carry out his evil plan for the prisoners.

On this road south of the South Loup River and near the Olive Ranch, Gillan and Dufran and the prisoners were met by Print and his men at the point where the trails forked, one leading to the Olive Ranch, the other to the Dufran Ranch up the valley.

---

[*] Current day Lexington

Holdup of the Officers by the Olive gang in Devil's Gap Canyon, December 10, 1878, and taking their prisoners, Mitchell and Ketchum, who were on their way to Custer County for trial. Re-enacted by S.D. Butcher, photographer and provided by the Nebraska State Historical Society Photograph Collections.

    A short consultation was held between Olive and the law officers. The consideration, what ever it was, was paid. It wasn't revealed how much but Bion Brown would testify later he saw a large roll of bills handed to Dufran.

    Gillan and Dufran got out of the wagon, mounted Olive's horses and rode to the Dufran Ranch. Dennis Gartrell, Olive's foreman, got off his horse and into the wagon, took the lines and drove back up the canyon a short distance. There a few rods from the trail, where a cluster of box elder and cottonwood trees stood, a trial of sorts was held for Mitchell and Ketchum.

    Bill Green again brought out the jugs, which were generously and frequently tipped. They staggered, speaking in unstable voices. Green drove the wagon under a leaning tree limb. A rope was thrown over it with a slip noose on both ends. Mitchell and Ketchum were ordered to stand up. A mock trial was held. Mitchell and Ketchum refused to answer any questions or make any statements. Gartrell stood in the wagon with them, holding the ends of the rope ready to slip over the heads of their victims as soon as Olive rendered a verdict.

    After Olive questioned the prisoners, Bill Green passed the jug around again. When the prisoners refused to answer questions, Gartrell put the loops over their heads. Ketchum held his head down with his chin close to his breast so it would be difficult to get the rope around his neck. Gartrell sawed the rope severely back and forth until he got it under Ketchum's chin and around his neck, remarking, "Damn you, I've got you where I want you now."

The hanging of Ketchum and Mitchell. Re-enacted by S.D. Butcher, photographer and provided by the Nebraska State Historical Society Photograph Collections.

The noose was finally slipped under his chin and slipped tight. The other noose was then put over Mitchell's head and tightened. Print, exasperated at getting no response, put the barrel of his rifle against Mitchell's body. "Damn you, why did you kill Bob?" Receiving no answer, he pulled the trigger. It blasted a hole in Mitchell's side and he fell back over the seat. Gartrell drove the wagon from under them leaving Mitchell and Ketchum hanging by their necks. No one seems to be quite certain how it happened, but sometime during the night the bodies were burned. One story is that Green and Baldwin, riding home late that night, stopped to offer the bodies a drink then dropped a match in the tinder-dry grass. Around the burned bodies a patch of grass also burned.

Boblits and McNamar left Custer City early the next morning to search for the prisoners. Others in the party who left town with the judge included Wamsgan, Able, Wise and George Sandford. They had spent the night in Custer City, expecting to be present for the hearing the next morning. All feared the worst for Mitchell and Ketchum. As they headed for Devil's Gap they could smell burned flesh and burned grass.

Following their nose they found the spot where Ketchum's body was hanging from the limb of a small tree and Mitchell's body on the ground with his wrist still handcuffed to Ketchum. Both bodies were burned beyond recognition. A small patch of grass was burned. The grass around was damp or this might have started a prairie fire, something most dreaded by all inhabitants. Boblits examined the bodies.

"Mitchell has been shot in the side," he stated. "This is probably the work of Print. If so, it was a terrible mistake on his part. These men could have been convicted easily and maybe hanged by Judge Gaslin. We'll ride to Plum Creek, get the sheriff and a coroner, and return."

Whether the bodies were burned accidentally or on purpose will never be fully known. Most people speculated that Green and Baldwin stopped on their way back, held a little party with the dead, tried to give them a drink, which spilled over the bodies. Somehow, there was a fire.

The next morning, Print Olive gave a cowhand $20 to bury the bodies. He found tough digging in the frozen ground so he dug a hole too small for the bodies. Mitchell's body was doubled up in a very bad shape with his hand pulled backward and over his head. He also severed one frozen arm and leg from Ketchum's body. They were buried so shallow that wolves scratched away the dirt and chewed on the flesh from the arm and breast of one body.

Conflicting stories roamed the "native telegraph."

Boblits told S. D. Butcher[*]:

"It is not known for certain where Gillan and Dufran stopped with the prisoners, but we think they stopped at the Dick James Ranch, the sheriff of Dawson County   All the details will never be known but we do know that on that very day, every detail of the arrangement was carried to the very letter."

Print Olive would soon learn that this horrible act will be his one sorry mistake. What might have been a quick trial; for murder and cattle stealing, with an easy conviction of Mitchell and Ketchum would turn into Nebraska's most famous murder trial, involving Print Olive and some of his men. An angry Judge William Gaslin would see to that. The story would rocket around the world and become front-page news in every newspaper.

---

[*] *The most accurate account comes through the S.D. Butcher's* History of Custer County, *who interviewed Judge Boblits and a cowboy named James Stockham. The author used this account to piece together the interviews of Boblits and Stockham. Stockham was a cowboy but never said he was an Olive employee.*

Showing the burned bodies of Mitchell and Ketchum, as photographed after being brought to Kearney. Courtesy of S.D. Butcher, photographer and Nebraska State Historical Photograph collections.

    Sheriff Dave Anderson with a coroner and posse, returned a day or so later, exhumed the bodies and laid them behind the mortuary in Kearney where they lay for days for all to see and examine. People looked, and left with utter contempt for Print Olive. There was talk of a lynch party on every street corner in every local town before he was caught.

CHAPTER EIGHT

Reining in the Frontier

"Horse stealin" is still no lost art in Nebraska," remarked Dilworth to Gaslin as he read the North Platte Nebraskan.

"On Friday night of last week some scoundrels stole two dark bay horses belonging to Fred Hanlon who lives about two miles east of this city. The mares are three and four years old, one branded with a half moon, and both have black feet.

"A reward of $50 is offered for their return and conviction of the thieves and we hope he has a chance to pay with the reward within a week.

"On Sunday night horse thieves broke into the stable of Joe Mackle on the south side and took two young stallions. The stable was locked, and the thieves acted as though they were perfectly familiar with the premises. Early Monday morning men were out searching for the stolen horses. One has been found that is thought to have escaped from the thieves. The other one has not been heard of. The two jobs were undoubtedly done by white men."

"No doubt some day the thieves will be in our court," answered Judge Gaslin as he and the attorney scheduled a circuit, "They never quit until they get caught."

Indians, small tribes not yet on reservations, were still masters of the art of stealing horses. And so it was always the hope of horse thieves that Indians would be blamed for the act. Doc Middleton had entered the horse-stealing arena, and of course when horses turned up missing, he was always under suspicion. He appeared, however, to prefer stealing horses from the Indian reservations in South Dakota and selling them to white men in northeastern Nebraska where he had made his home. That is, after the Indians had stolen the horses from the big outfit's roundup, the herd of horses from which those to be used for the day are chosen.

When it got too hot for Tony Pastor, a notorious horse thief, and it looked as if he would be tried in a Gaslin court, he rode across the line into Wyoming, arriving in Cheyenne.

It was assumed it was the same Pastor who once arrived in St. Paul, Nebraska, from the Black Hills about five months before in the company of Con Coutier, also an outlaw.

A vigilante committee caught up with Pastor near Cheyenne and hanged him. The Platte Valley Independent said it "was for his weakness of carrying off halters with other men's horses attached thereto; it is a consummation most devoutly to be wished for that Con may be speedily sent to keep Tony company."

Thus the state of Nebraska was saved some money and Judge Gaslin lots of work.

Maybe he was taken to the Buffalo County jail, to be tried by Judge Gaslin. The Platte Valley Independent reported him as the "latest of fresh arrivals of horse thieves to be brought to Kearney."

Just a month before, Sheriff J.D. Dreary caught one more horse thief, D. Gordon in Franklin County. Gordon had been tried in Judge Whittier's Franklin County Court and sentenced to thirty days in jail for a minor charge. This time he was arrested for stealing a horse from a Franklin County farmer. He might have escaped, but he wanted to see his wife once more before he departed and arranged for a meeting with her at an appointed place in the eastern part of the county. His wife didn't keep the engagement but the sheriff "appeared as a substitute promptly on time."

The noose or Gaslin's court seemed to take care of most of the horse thieves sooner or later. In spite of all this, Doc Middleton still ran free and more confident than ever than he would be hard to catch.

The Lincoln Journal, speaking of the twenty-six murders in three years in Judge Gaslin's Fifth District said, "This is twice as many murders as all the other districts in the state combined and, verily, is a bad showing for the district.

"The judge always inflicts the most severe penalties that the law allows according to the verdict. He is an excellent judge for such a district and could do much to decrease crime if he could always get juries willing to do their duty and mete out punishment according to the nature of the offense. The time for showing mercy to criminals and thereby putting a premium upon crime ought to be in the past."

Still 1878

Judge Gaslin lies back in his passenger seat on a train headed for Sidney. He was tired and needed rest, but wasn't getting much as he watched the scenery go by. Cattle grazed contently in the river valley. This didn't help; it only reminded him of the trouble brewing over rustling and murder cases sure to come up in western Nebraska trials.

He had difficult trials in Nebraska City and was anticipating even more difficult trials in Sidney, some for murder. He was discouraged; he seemed to be making so little headway in his battle to bring a semblance of order to his far-reaching Fifth District.

It all kept reminding him of the coming trial of Mitchell and Ketchum for the murder of Bob Olive, alias Stevens, to be held in Custer City of Custer County. The two accused were to be taken to that city for trial, to be held as soon as he returned from Sidney. He had tried to bring peace between these parties.

His thoughts were interrupted by the conductor bringing him a telegram -"Olives hang, burn Mitchell and Ketchum on way to Custer City- stop. Have sheriffs bluffed out," sighed Dilworth.

Judge Gaslin was furious. His anger smoldered. Knowing Print Olive and his hot temper, he knew he would have to have a foolproof plan to bring him to justice. He looked out the window at the pine-studded hills to the south; then closed his eyes to work out a plan. What sympathy he had left for Olive and his problems with cattle rustlers had evaporated.

He knew how difficult it would be to arrest Print and his men. Later he told Custer County historian and early photographer, S. D. Butcher, of how he planned for the capture of the "Olive Gang" as he called them.

"I first heard of the lynching of Mitchell and Ketchum while on a train on my way from Nebraska City to Sidney where I was to open court the next morning. When I opened court there was such an excitement that there was no disposition or readiness to do business. Upon seeing an article in the newspaper published at Kearney by the Eatons, denouncing the governor for not taking active steps to bring about the arrest of the murderers and complimenting me by saying that there was only one man in Nebraska who could see that the perpetrators of the crime would be brought to justice, and that man was Gaslin, I called my court reporter, F. M. Hallowell, who was on assignment. I instructed him to proceed to Kearney on the first train and tell Eaton not to make further mention of my name in connection with the matter, as I had a plan to capture the desperadoes and did not want my name mentioned for fear of putting them on their guard. Late that afternoon I adjourned court and took the train east to Plum Creek[*] where quite a number of the Olive gang lived.

"I found assembled at the residence of Attorney General Dilworth a number of law abiding citizens of the city, armed to protect themselves against the outlaws who had threatened the lives of those who should attempt to bring them to justice. Among these, I now recall an attorney, Captain McNamar, and Jack MacColl, clerk of the district court. I learned that all the officials of Custer County, where the lynching was done, either belonged to or were under the influence of the Olive gang. And, as they could not be moved against, by or through any of the officials of that county, I left on the first train for Kearney to look up the law. I wanted to see if I, as an examining magistrate, could issue warrants for their arrest, which plan I divulged to no one.

"I was in constant touch with General Dilworth, and soon satisfied myself that I had the authority. I set to work preparing complaints and warrants to have the outlaws arrested. After I had matured my plans, I met J. P. Johnson, and in conversation he remarked that if the officers were afraid to arrest the criminals he would furnish men to do it if I would deputize them.

"I informed him I had confidentially arranged for a meeting of the sheriffs of Dawson and Buffalo Counties, General Dilworth and a sacred few others, and invited him to attend. There were present at this meeting in Judge Savidge's office the Judge, J. P. Johnson, General Dilworth, the two sheriffs and myself. I told these men the conclusions I had come to, and the complaints having been filed before me, I made out the warrants for the arrest of the criminals and offered them to Sheriff James of Dawson County and Sheriff Anderson of Buffalo County. Both of them declined to take or serve

---

[*] Renamed Lexington

them on account of a fear for their lives.

"I then turned to Johnson and asked him to give me the names of the men he agreed to furnish, which he did, and I deputized them. There were, I think, five or six of them, and I gave the warrants to Johnson for delivery. One of the men deputized was Lawrence Ketchum, a brother of the man who was lynched, and another was a powerful young fellow by the name of Young, a deputy sheriff of Clay County. A third man was named Pinegree, and a fourth was a man from Illinois."

Gaslin deputized several of the above-mentioned men to go cross-country to the Olive ranch and arrest whomever was there. These men did do this but they found the Olive men had escaped. Probably they saw them coming and left through the high back doors of the barn and rode into the hills. [*]

Then Gaslin implemented his second plan--arrest the men in Plum Creek. Learning, through Dilworth, that all of them were in Plum Creek, he ordered Dilworth to take his crew there and arrest Olive and his gang. Locally, another group of men stood ready to help, armed with thirty Needle Guns.

Dilworth and his men left Kearney on the Union Pacific Railroad early Saturday morning, all well armed with rifles and revolvers. His gang included Lawrence, Samuel and Larch Ketchum, brothers of Ami, and angry enough to hang the men to the nearest tree or telegraph pole. Others were J. K. and B. F. Moury, a man named Shepherd and Samuel Snow.[**]

They were greeted by a large body of local citizens in Plum Creek gathered on Main Street, discussing how the murderers might be caught and hanged. This made Dilworth nervous, and he hoped this would not alert Olive and his gang. His men scattered out to carefully and quietly capture Olive and his men.

---

[*] *Author's note: Why do I think this? While editor of the* Platte Valley Farmer-Stockman *in Cozad, the author interviewed 90-year-old Mrs. Meyers in Callaway who told of visiting the Olive ranch with her father. She told of the barn with high, large doors back and front, so designed that a man could ride in or out without dismounting.*

[**] *Brother of Tamar Snow's father, perhaps?*

Dilworth made a deal with the postmaster to hide Larch, Lawrence and himself in the mailroom. He carefully instructed the Ketchums not to get trigger happy if Print walked in.

Just when Dilworth began to think the wanted men had been alerted and either hid or left town, in walked Armstrong, limping. (He had been wounded in the leg by one of Ketchum's or Mitchell's shots as the men rode from the battleground.)

Dilworth nodded to Lawrence who quietly slipped through the door. When Armstrong saw Lawrence he went for his gun; then changed his mind. He started to curse Lawrence but when he heard the click of the hammer on Lawrence's needle-gun, he raised his hands high.

Lawrence motioned him to the back room. There Dilworth whispered in no uncertain words "You better keep your mouth shut and not make a sound," and enforced his edict at the point of his Winchester which also had a trigger cocked. Then Print walked in unarmed.

"Good morning, Print," greeted the postmaster.

"Tom, I need a doctor bad. My baby is sick. I can't find a...."

Laron walked out, needle-gun in hand, cocked and pointed at Print. "Put up your hands and come with me," whispered Laron and steered Print to the back room.

"Tom, will you find a doctor and send him up to the house?" asked Print.

"Sure will," answered the postmaster.

Print started to curse Dilworth; then quietly submitted to the handcuffs after he felt a gun barrel in his back in the hands of Laron.

The last to walk in was Bion Brown. He, too, was unarmed. Lawrence arrested him without incident. John Baldwin was captured at his home. Other men caught Green in bed. Fisher was caught on Main Street.

Dilworth gathered the arrested men and chained them together by twos. He put them on the eastbound train and arrested John Gatlin, one of Olive's herders, in a bar in Elm Creek.

Interestingly, Armstrong was the only man to carry a gun. Why there were no guns is a good question. It was against the law in many towns to carry guns inside the city limits. They could be left with the sheriff or with a bartender. Print probably left his at home.

Sheriff Gillan was arrested Monday night in Plum Creek and brought to Kearney, making twelve in all to be arrested.

CHAPTER NINE

The Gavel and The Gun

1879

Meantime horror stories of the murder and the burning of the bodies traveled nationwide and only served to heat up the passions of those who wanted to hate the Olives anyway.

This letter appeared in the <u>Platte Valley Independent,</u> a Grand Island newspaper. It was an example of how stories are enhanced as they travel via the "frontier telegraph".

<u>An Open letter from a Kearney woman to Print Olive,</u> December 28,1878:

> Sir: It is with fear and trembling that I venture to address you with these lines of pity and remonstrance. But, being a woman, I do not believe people should burn men at the stake as you did poor Ketchum and Mitchell. You have had a terrible revenge on your victims--such revenge as the devil in hell only could have conceived. No human being living, besides you, could have conceived of such a fiendish and brutal revenge.
>
> These two unfortunate men were killed by a desperado named "Stevens" (AKA Bob Olive) under circumstances palliating if not justifiable. This desperado had killed two men in Texas and was living with you under an assumed name. He is believed to be your own brother.
>
> He recently committed two penitentiary offences in Kearney, by shooting at a citizen and by drawing a pistol on the marshal. He was let off without due punishment, as our town officers were afraid to punish him, for they feared him. This murderer swore out an affidavit against Ketchum for alleged cattle stealing and was deputized by our sheriff to arrest Ketchum. It is well known that Stevens and Ketchum were sworn enemies. This lawless desperado was clothed with

expected Ketchum to surrender to his sworn enemy. Then you came to Kearney with the dead body of your brother and publicly offered $1,000 reward for Mitchell and Ketchum, dead or alive. You swore eternal vengeance, you scattered telegrams and postal cards all over the state and set the law hounds after blood. The two men made no attempt to escape but quietly surrendered only asking for a fair trial.

The other sheriffs of Merrick and Howard Counties knew...they knew you had sworn to kill these two men and they are bound to you for the mercenary ties of blood money. You need have no fear of the sheriffs, as they will never attempt to bring you to justice. You are known to be an infamous, cowardly and unscrupulous desperado, and our sheriffs will give you wide birth.

You have established a reign of terror in the Loup Country and men fear you. But mark my prediction. The blood of Mitchell and Ketchum is crying for vengeance. Your blood alone can atone for these great wrongs. The very stones cry out against you, Hell yawns for you; heaven weeps at the sight of such a villainous beast as you are in human form. The devil's fires are blazing brighter in anticipation of your speedy coming.

The indignant and terrified homesteaders of the Loup will not long tolerate the presence of such a cowardly assassin as you are. Wealthy and wicked, savage and cowardly as you are, you may well tremble for your miserable life ... From a woman in Kearney.

Meanwhile rumors of bribery offers by Olive began to circulate. The <u>Kearney Press</u> offered this opinion:

There have been rumors in circulation for several days that an attempt has been made to bribe certain persons connected with the Olive trial. One of these rumors even went to the extent of declaring that a definite offer had been made to a member of the preliminary hearing (petit jury) proposing to pay him $1,000 cash if he should be one of the men drawn to try Print Olive. As a consideration he was to pledge himself to vote each time in favor of acquitting Olive and thereby compel a disagreement of the jury even if an acquittal could not be obtained.

Judge Gaslin heard these rumors, too, and addressed the Grand Jury. "I have a case to present to this body which is different from anything that has ever come to my judicial knowledge since I have been on the bench. Evidence has been presented to make it appear that an attempt at bribery has been committed, and the jury should examine the evidence and take action thereon."

The Grand Jury immediately summoned witnesses and that afternoon returned an indictment, which confirmed the rumor. The guilty juror was dismissed at once.

The Grand Jury quickly returned an indictment against I. P. Olive, William H. Green, John Baldwin, Frederick Fisher, Bion Brown, Barney J. Gillan, Pedro Dominicus, Phillip DuFran and Dennis Gartrell. It read: "The Indictment charges Olive and his partners in shooting Mitchell with a rifle, then hanging him and burning him. Trial to begin March 1, 1879."

However, the judge changed the trial date to April 15. Judge Gaslin also ruled that the trial be held in Hastings, rather than in Custer County. Custer County was still unorganized and there was no place there to hold what had now become such a famous trial. He would no longer consider the Olive barn.

Perhaps the delay was at the request of the defense to allow Print's father, James Olive, to arrive from Texas to aid his son in his murder trial.

The <u>Omaha News</u> interviewed the elder Olive when he arrived by train in Omaha:

> *Among the passengers at the westbound train was James Olive, an I. W. Olive, father, mother and brother of I. P. Olive of Plum Creek.[*] Accompanying them was J. Wood, better known as "Happy Jack", a herder from Plum Creek. They came from Williamson County, Texas, where on the Little Brushy Creek, the old gentleman owns thousands of acres, thousands of cattle and hundreds of horses. The father is short, slightly bent with age. He has passed his seventy-eighth birth date but is still hale and hearty and says he can drive a knife to the hilt if necessary. Mrs. Olive is fourteen years younger. Ira W. is in prime of life.*
>
> *They are on their way to Olive's ranch to take charge of his large*

---

[*] Renamed Lexington

property and manage his interests while he is on trial for murder. They plan to publish and circulate a testimony of the past life of I. P. Olive that would entirely disprove the reckless and extravagant stories, which have been freely sent broadcast to do him injury. The testimonial had been prepared and was attested by the county officials under seal.

Some three years ago a neighbor named Fringe (taken from this testimonial), was driving cattle, a few Olive cattle mixed in. He asked where he should cut their cattle off, to which Olive replied "At the ford." He passed the ford, however, without complying with his promise and was overtaken by the boys. When Jay Olive said, "Those are some of Prentices cattle" Fringe denied this but, on their being pointed out to him, he merely said. "I'll see you when the leaves are on the trees" and drove on.

A few weeks later he waylaid Jay Olive and shot him through the hat but failed to kill him. Jay, a quiet man, did not return the fire, but let the man pass.

Shortly after Print met Fringe and called him to account for shooting at his brother. Fringe, becoming angry, told him that he had shot at Jay and "would like to get at you, too. Both men drew revolvers and began firing. Olive was shot four times and Fringe three times. Prince, (as his father called him) was unable to leave the spot but lie on the ground until his brothers came and took him home. Fringe crept off into the brush until the brothers had gone. After he was taken home, he died. Prince recovered. From this time the Olive boys were threatened and friends of Fringe made threats that the Olives should not escape with their lives.

One night, about one o'clock, when the boys had been working in the branding pens all day, the brothers and a colored man employee were lying asleep on the piazza, it being very warm. The Fringe outfit stole up on them and fired into the party, intending to kill every man there. However, a bundle of dry hides, laying near them deceived the assailants and a portion of their shots were lost in the hides. Prince was shot through the shoulder and leg, the black man twice in the face and Jay was shot twenty times. He crept off in the darkness and Prince got out of sight. But the negro was caught and made to light a fence board and look for the boys under threats from the murderous ranchers. After the affair, I. P. Olive left Texas and came north, it *being evident that to stay in that neighborhood was courting death.*

These are the facts James Olive was to have published if the town of Taylor, Texas had not been burned.

******

There was no courthouse in Hastings, so the trial was to be held in what was called Liberal Hall. On Sunday it served as a church. Adams County voters had wrenched the county seat from Juniata but voters would not vote money for a new courthouse. Gaslin had decided to try only two men for the murder---I. P. Olive and Frederick Fisher. He feared for the lives of the men from lynch mobs so he had them kept in the Clay County jail at Clay Center. Bion Brown had turned state's evidence but he was also jailed with Olive and Fisher. There, by previous agreement, he was to listen to all the conversations and report each day by arrangement with the sheriff to John M. Thurston, one of the attorneys for the prosecution (later Nebraska state senator).

Brown, kept Thurston informed of plans and schemes of the Olives and his part in the matter of their proposed rescue, and Thurston kept Gaslin advised. "Their attorneys keep advising them we can't get a conviction unless someone in their party turns state's evidence, and their advice is probably correct. These attorneys therefore are urging Olive and associates not to attempt anything desperate, or at least refrain from doing so until it becomes certain that some of their party is to be called as a witness."

Thurston and Dilworth were apprehensive about death threats against the judge and the prosecution. Cowboys, as cowboys often did when they came to town, got high on whiskey and rode through the streets of Hastings whooping and yelling, and shooting off revolvers. This made Dilworth nervous but he was not unduly concerned. But, after Brown had given such condemning evidence, Thurston began to fear for his life and the lives of Gaslin and Dilworth. Every day of the trial the cowboys were there, guns banging against chairs when they sat down, action not designed to make the jury and the judge more comfortable. Those standing made sure their guns stocks could be noticed. The judge each day laid out his revolvers but he knew it was more of a bluff than any protection from 200 cowboys firing at the bench.

"That night (before the trial began) was one of the most sensational and exciting I ever passed through," said Thurston. "Countless numbers of cowboys riding and roaming about town, many of them drinking and making all sorts of threats as to what would happen.

"Bion Brown had already informed me that if any of the defendants should be called by the state as a witness, the cowboys were to fill up the building of the court then raise up in a body and commence shooting. Their instructions being to kill the judge and attorney general and not to shoot me if it could be avoided.

"The latter part of these directions gave me no consolation, for I knew if two or three hundred cowboys were shooting in the room, I was apt, even perhaps more apt, to be hit than someone they were shooting at."

Jury selection took a couple of days. The trial began in earnest April 15.

By the time all the cowboys, 200 strong, crowded into the court room, plus newspaper reporters sent from Omaha and Lincoln and from one national paper, there was little room left for common spectators.

Ira T. Paine, attorney in Grand Island, thought his son, Bayard H., should experience the famous trial. He borrowed a covered wagon, drove to Hastings and camped near Liberal Hall. Early the first morning of the trial they were among the first to enter the courtroom and secured a seat right up front. "Listen closely," whispered the father to his l0-year-old son, "This will be a great learning experience for you."

Judge Gaslin looked down from his bench and smiled at the boy. Then his eyes returned to the gun-toting cowboys, trying to detect signs that they might use their guns to interrupt the court. He loosened his tie, **took his own two revolvers from his brief case, cocked the triggers** and laid them in full view on the bench. The cowboys, bleary eyed from rampaging the night before, eyed the judge as well. Of course not all were Olive cowboys but it was evident they were sympathetic to his cause.

Olive's wife, Louisa, sat in front, her small child in her arms. Once she had tried to urge Print to put away his arms, as they were no longer needed, especially for protection from Indians who were now on reservations. He told her "there are still plenty of cattle rustlers left out there." She now wiped a tear from her eyes now and then. Her baby, still ill, cried frequently and she tried to comfort him. Also there were Print's father, James Olive from Texas, and his brother Ira. Ira Olive was the gentle person of the family and never seemed to have any trouble. He also ranched in the area and lived in Plum Creek. After the bailiff had called court into session, William Gaslin called the court to order.

"I have postponed all other trials until this one is consummated," he stated before beginning the trial.

The trial had not progressed long before the prosecuting attorney secretly informed Gaslin that he had made a secret arrangement with Bion Brown to turn state's evidence, to testify on behalf of the prosecution. Brown, in jail with the other defendants, heard and knew all their plans, and daily communicated the same to General Dilworth, the prosecuting attorney, and to the sheriff.

Brown told Dilworth that at one time the Olives had talked of having their friends, who were in disguise in town, shoot Dilworth and have horses ready for the prisoners, who would be enabled to escape in the excitement.

The Judge gave orders for no one to occupy the gallery opposite where he sat and he had a large number of bailiffs, heavily armed, secretly scattered throughout the courtroom, with nothing to indicate they were officers. One day it was reported to Dilworth that a number of Texas friends of the prisoners were secreted in the hills near the Platte River, armed to the teeth, and provided with good horses with which to swoop down on the court and liberate the prisoners.

Brown, as a first witness, swore that he saw Olive give Sheriff Gillan money, but didn't know how much. "Pedro, Gartrell, Kelley and I were at the Olive Ranch on December 10 (records show Dec. 9) when Fisher came up on horseback and told us that Olive wanted us to meet him on the banks of Wood River.

"As we neared we heard hollering and whistling for us to come on. The man was Olive. All of us went to Devil's Gap on the South Loup River. There we met the wagon with the prisoners, Mitchell and Ketchum, who were with DuFran and Gillan.

"Olive demanded the prisoners from Gillan who said he hated to give them up, but finally yielded. Gartrell then jumped into the wagon and seized the reins. DuFran and Gillan got out and went back some three or four hundred yards. Olive rode to an elm tree nearby but, after examining it, said it would not 'answer' as it was too large. Having found a smaller one, which suited his purpose, he ordered the wagon containing Mitchell and Ketchum to be driven under it.

"When that was done Gartrell put a rope around Ketchum's neck and the Mexican Pedro served Mitchell in like manner. The ropes were then tied to a limb of the tree and the prisoners handcuffed (together). Olive stood by the wagon. Mitchell was in the bottom of the floor of the wagon box and Ketchum leaned slightly over the side.

"Olive grabbed a Winchester rifle and shot Mitchell in the right side. The wounded man fell back over the wheel. Gartrell and Olive then got into the wagon together. Gartrell took up the lines and drove the wagon under the tree. The clothing of the wounded man caught fire from the gunfire and I was ordered to put out the fire. After that Olive walked to the wagon and took a drink of whiskey. Green and Baldwin exchanged horses with the Mexican and me and started back to Plum Creek."

Under cross examination, Brown again testified positively that he saw Olive pay money to Sheriff Gillan and that Olive, Fisher, Green, Baldwin, Gartrell, the Mexican and he were present at the hanging.

Brown testified that he was twenty-one years of age, a native of Ohio. He was called good looking, with a frank, open-face and had been in the employ of Olive for ten months. He testified "I was compelled by Olive at the point of a gun to assist in the lynching of Mitchell and Ketchum."

Those assembled in the courtroom with Judge Gaslin included the Sheriff of Adams County, Marshal of Hastings, Lieutenant Governor of the state, E. C. Cams, and the Secretary of State, S. J. Alexander.

All the above joined in telegrams to the governor at Lincoln urging government assistance in preventing the defendants from making an attack on the court.

Governor Nance burned up the wires to Washington, and about three o'clock, word was received that a party of two regular infantry would leave Ft. Omaha by five or six in the morning and would reach Hastings about l0 a.m.

Gaslin opened court the next morning, knowing a crisis was at hand. He asked Thurston to take delaying action.

"Say anything, just keep talking until the army arrives," urged the judge. "They may wait until you sit down so as to get a clear shot at Dilworth and me."

Thurston stood up and made a motion, although it was not an important one. But it was only to give him something to talk about at length. He droned on and on, not sticking to the subject very well. He paced before the bench as he talked to protect the judge and district attorney. An hour passed, then two hours. The impatient young Paine wondered what kind of a trial this was going to be. The elder Paine winked at him and whispered, "Just wait."

At nine o'clock there were no signs of the soldiers and Thurston was running of out of steam. He took a drink of water and stared at the cowboys. At 10 o'clock he was still speaking but hustling for words. He smiled acknowledgment to the elder Paine, a friend, and continued. But he was getting desperate and turned to the judge for help. He looked at his watch. It was 10:45 a.m. "As you know, this will be the most celebrated trial in this young state's history and ---."

A bugle blew outside, Uncle Sam's bugle. He looked at the judge and smiled. He thought - that is the sweetest music I will ever hear in my life! Gaslin put his guns aside.

Without waiting for a court recess, everyone rushed from the courtroom into the street. There, coming up the street, was what Thurston called "the finest sight that my eyes have ever fallen on: 92 regulars, marching with steady steps with a Gatling Gun and guard, and at the their heads was the man we used to call Little Andy Burt, a captain in the regular army and, over all, the old flag."

On came the 92 regulars and deployed upon a vacant block diagonally across from the courtroom. Ammunition was passed out and the Gatling Gun squad stood ready for action. The other soldiers began making camp.

Said Thurston later: "I never saw so surprised and so quiet a crowd of men in my life as those cowboys. They would have cheerfully attacked 500 militiamen, but not 92 regular with a Gatling Gun and the flag. Little Andy Burt in command put the fear of God into them in two seconds. Trouble was over. We went back into the court room."

Thurston immediately withdrew his motion and called for witness Bion Brown to continue.

The next morning the judge issued an order: no guns in the courtroom. All must be left at the door with the sheriff. Gaslin left his guns in his brief case.

The defense, headed by James Laird, called on John Dyer, Samuel Ritchie, E. S. Finch, A. R. Brodney, John Hoffman, William Kilgore, and Coe and his wife.

Hoffman –"I saw twelve or fifteen horsemen pass the DuFran Ranch after dark the evening of December 10. They were going towards Devil's Gap, where the men were hanged."

Finch – "I saw, before sunset, a party of six men on horseback pass my ranch going towards DuFran's Ranch, which is 12 miles away."

Dyer – "On that same day, at a point ten miles south of the Finch Ranch and seven miles from Devil's Gap, I saw fifteen or twenty armed horsemen riding toward the gap."

None of the witnesses said they recognized any in the party seen by them.

Coe and his wife, and Kilgore - all testified that DuFran told them on Christmas Day that he himself didn't know any of the men who took Ketchum and Mitchell from Gillan and himself and that there were fifteen or twenty men in the company.

Brodney - Also testified that DuFran told him at Plum Creek[*] on March 5 that he didn't know the crowd that took the prisoners away.

Ritchie - Confirmed DuFran's testimony.

The object of introducing these witnesses was to impeach Brown's testimony. The defense rested, then moved to strike DuFran and Brown's testimony on the grounds that being under indictment for the same offences as that charged against Olive and Fisher, that they are not competent witnesses against the defendants. Gaslin overruled these motions.

George Sanford, witness for defense ....said he lived with Anton Abel two miles from Custer City, the county seat. He said the men were hung with 7/8-inch rope and he confirmed former testimony that Mitchell's rope was burned off and he was in

---

[*] Current day Lexington

a sitting position and fastened to Ketchum by handcuffs. "Mitchell's body was so badly burned that, when lifted, one leg fell off at the knee. The fire burned a circle of three to four feet in diameter. I examined the ashes, and there were no wood ashes. The site is about a quarter of a mile from the forks in the road, one of which goes to the Olive Ranch and one to the Abel Ranch.

The defense called a series of character witnesses to establish Olive's character as a peaceable and law abiding citizen. All, of course, pronounced his reputation in Custer County as good. Those acquainted with him in Dawson County spoke of him as a square, fair, honest man and one with whom they have had no trouble.

Some had been with him on roundups and had never known him to be quarrelsome. Several had heard of frequent difficulties in which he had become involved and had heard of him drawing his revolver on several men. Those who had claimed to know anything of the difficulties expressed themselves as of the opinion that he was provoked, so to warrant his assault with the revolver.

Laird called A. W. Woodworth for the defense. "I live thirty miles northeast of Custer City. Armstrong, I am told, was instructed to say to small cattle dealers and farmers that Olive would deal fairly with them and that he was authorized to settle for any damages done, and I know him to be a law abiding man and of good character."

The attorneys on both sides got into an argument.
"Is not this Armstrong under indictment as accessory to the offence of these men on trial?" asked prosecutor Thurston.

Laird .... "Wait, we object. It makes no difference whether he is under indictment or not. You have the whole county under indictment."

Thurston ...."We shall have conviction on them, too."

Laird ...."I guess before you have accomplished that, you will hear from us. We propose to be on hand at your funeral procession when it comes.."

Gaslin sat upright in his chair. "Now gentlemen..."
Laird interrupts.
Laird---"Armstrong has rights even if he is indicted, although it would seem that no one is entitled to any rights in this court."

Judge Gaslin - "Mr. Laird, the court fines you $25 for contempt of court and you are ordered into the custody of the sheriff until the fine is paid."

Laird made a fiery and eloquent speech for a few moments and when he took his seat a little applause started in the back of the room. The bailiffs soon quelled the disturbance.

Hamer, defense attorney, with a few well-chosen and temperate remarks denounced the action of the court, and said he feared the case would be prejudiced. "I think the intentions of Laird and purport of his language has been misjudged."

Gaslin - "I have no feelings, no passion in the matter, I have not been out of humor in the least the past two days. This is one of the saddest things I ever did in my life. I don't care what men say about me individually and out of the courtroom. But a court is a place where men come to have justice done them.

"A court should be run in an orderly and gentlemanly manner, I have importuned counsel in the case to refrain from bickering. I have borne everything. It has been years since I have entertained the least animosity or ill feeling toward any man and I bear none either to the defendants or the counsel. In this case I think I am called upon to discharge a solemn duty. I do it with sadness."

Defense attorney Corrigan then spoke on behalf of Laird. He thought he had been goaded into the remarks by the opposing counsel. The judge was not impressed and restated his remonstrance against Laird.

"The court finds James Laird guilty of disrespectful, contemptuous and insolent behavior and language toward the court, in wrangling and using rude and boisterous language to opposing counsel and to the court. And among other things, he speaks in a contemptuous, rude and insolent manner to the court. He further stated that 'It seems that no one has any rights in this court.' Therefore, I fined Laird $25 for contempt."

Laird again tried to get Judge Gaslin to change his mind, leaving out the words "in this court". Gaslin refused. Laird left the courtroom and did not return for the rest of the day.

April 17, court resumed; Judge William Gaslin cautioned the defense about entering any testimony involving Ketchum and the assumption that he had stolen cattle or about his killing of Stevens

(Bob Olive). "That has no bearing or place in this trial."

Nevertheless, the defense kept bringing up various items. Such as: whether Ketchum was a cattle thief. Whether stockmen have suffered losses by thieves to a great extent. Whether the cattlemen has had losses worth $10,000 in stolen livestock. Whether Ketchum killed twenty-five head of Olive cattle in one day. Whether cattlemen have any protection against cattle stealing unless they protect themselves. Doc Middleton and his band of horse thieves were mentioned. Each time, the prosecution objected and the judge upheld their objections; nevertheless the thought was presented to the jury and may have contributed to a lesser verdict than first-degree murder.

April 18. The trial ended and Judge Gaslin read his statement to the jury, instructing them what to consider before they reached a verdict. He placed Olive and Fisher in the custody of the U.S. Army.

April 19---After eighteen hours of deliberation, the jury returned a verdict of guilty of murder in the second degree. Judge Gaslin sentenced Olive and Fisher to life in the penitentiary at hard labor.

"All kinds of lawyers, good or bad, were employed by the defense," said Judge Gaslin later, "some for ability and legal lore, and some to insult and bulldoze the Court."

Pedro Dominicus also served as a witness for the prosecution. "A better witness I never heard testify, even though he had to testify through an interpreter," said Gaslin.

The Omaha Republican did not think the trial was fair:

How about the verdict? Who weakened? Who was obstinate? Can it be that money brought about the final agreement?

> The jurors stood on the first ballot ten for murder in the first degree, one for second degree and one for manslaughter, reported this newspaper. The verdict was considered for seventeen hours. The verdict was the result of compromise. West voted on the first ballot for murder the second degree and Thomas Carroll voted for manslaughter. The remaining ten held firmly to their opinion until one by one they became convinced that their

> two obstinate companions would not yield and, rather than have a hung jury, reluctantly acquiesced in the compromise of second degree murder.
>
> Undoubtedly the statements of opinions by the attorneys concerning the killing of Stevens (Olive) and the stealing of cattle, although properly ruled out as evidence by Judge Gaslin, had their effect and assisted in bringing about the final verdict. Thomas Carroll remarked to the newspaper reporter as he left the courtroom, "I thought the extreme penalty for murder in the second degree was twelve to fifteen years in the pen, at the option of the judge, which I thought was enough. Had I known it would be made for life, I never would have signed that verdict in God's world."

The defendants decided to take their case to the Supreme Court. "We will fight until hell freezes over," said Print's father, James Olive. None of the other men were brought to trial.

Now that the trial of Olive was over, a woman in Texas felt it was safe to write a letter to the editor of her local Texas newspaper. The headlines read:

Print and Bob Olive, the worst men that ever lived in Texas.

The Platte Valley Independent reprinted the letter from the Taylorsville (Texas) Times, March 1, 1879:

> "For some weeks past the Northern papers have been teeming with reports of the burning at the stake of Ketchum and Mitchell, in Nebraska, in which Prentice "Print" Olive, formerly of this county, figures as a demon of the most damnable hue.
>
> "We solemnly protest against having any odium resting upon the fair fame of our state, or her people by reasons of the dark deeds of this monster in human shape; for even while a resident among us he was not a citizen, but an outlaw. Two years ago he left this section to insure his personal safety, after narrowly escaping death at the hands of the many whom he robbed or otherwise wronged. There is scarcely a crime in the calendar with which he is not charged by many of our oldest and most worthy citizens.
>
> "At the close of the late war the Olive family had nothing whatever but a very few head of stock, but under Print's management their

herds increased to magnificent proportions. In the same ratio the herds of their neighbors grew less. Fierce and savage and brutal, he was feared by all and thus he was able to defy all opposition, even of officers and courts and juries. His boasted motto was that it was "easier to move men than cattle," a principle, which he always fully lived up to, as his many acts of savage intimidation and red-handed murder, will attest.

"There were, of course, occasional conflicts with other stockmen, but having gathered around him a large party of desperate men, Print always came out the victor. Finally a score or more brave desperate men met and determined that this tyrannical sway of the Olive party should end, and their red-handed rule broken forever. With what success their resolves were attended is too well known. Suffice to say that one of the brothers, Jay Olive, was killed and Print nearly met the same fate. He was wounded but not very seriously.

"Now it was that they saw the intensity of popular feeling, and realized that the avenging hand of a fearfully outraged community would soon fasten its death grip upon them if they longer remained here; so they moved to Nebraska, taking with them their large stock of cattle valued at $100,000.

"The killing of Deets Phreme was a crime for which Olive and his associates should have forfeited their own lives, but at the time their power was greater than that of the law. By intimidating witnesses they were enabled to get a verdict of acquittal. Deets was a young man from Salado, Bell County, of good standing and well respected. He moved to this county in 1875, and engaged in cattle raising. Several months after being here Print and Bob Olive and party, who in a very savage manner charged him with the killing of their cattle, met him on the prairie. After clubbing him over the head with their six-shooters, released him and told him the next time they caught him on the prairie they would kill him.

"Poor Phreme's whole interest lay on the prairies he was met a few days later by Print Olive and his party and shot down in cold blood. He fought bravely for his life and in the fight wounded Print Olive, but the odds mere too great and the green grass was soon dyed crimson by his blood.

"It is charged that Bob Olive murdered a negro whom he had in his employ, named John Kelley, For no other reason than that he, Kelley, was too familiar with the villainous deeds of the Olives, and might someday "blow" on them. For this murder he was indicted in the district court of this county, and but a few days before his trial was to be held, he deliberately murdered Dock Kelley, brother of John, to destroy his testimony, as he was a witness against him for the killing of his brother. The first murder occurred in 1875, the second murder in 1876.

"Bob Olive was now declared an outlaw, but he managed to evade arrest and soon added another victim to his list. Apparently, without provocation, he shot and killed Cal Nutt, in a saloon in McDade. To this day the motive for this killing is wrapped in mystery, except for the demon's natural thirst for blood.

"In the year 1876 two negroes, said to be from Liberty, Texas, disappeared after having been last seen in the Olive neighborhood. A few days afterwards two other negroes, friends of the missing two, went into the Olive neighborhood in search of their lost friends. They were captured by Print and Bob Olive and were told they had no business prowling around that neighborhood and that they should be killed for this unpardonable indiscretion. The negroes say they were taken to the Olive store, and while the Olives were holding a consultation in the store, they made a bold break for liberty and thus escaped the murder these fiends were preparing for them. A short time subsequently, the bodies of the two missing Negroes from Liberty were found in a ravine in Dry Bushy Creek in the Olive neighborhood.

"Again, in 1876 two negroes, Red Banks and Jack Dodson, stopped at Print's house, on one of the main roads of the county, and asked if they could alight from their horses get a drink of water from the well. Mrs. Olive kindly granted their request but while the negroes were getting the water, Print Olive, who was in the rear of the house, rushed furiously upon the negroes and before they could explain their presence, shot Red Banks and shot at Dodson as he was making a hasty and successful retreat.

"But, by far the darkest and most damnable deed committed by these blood hounds was the whipping and killing of young Smith, a mere boy not exceeding sixteen years of age. In his innocence he was wending his way through the fatal precincts of the Olive neighborhood. Suddenly, he was confronted by Print Olive and his dirty, murderous menials who demanded to know his business. The boy, alarmed and terrified, explained as best his frightened condition would permit, but the savages, through their polluted vision, imagined he was a spy from the enemy's camp. They set upon him with their heavy riding whips and in the presence of a respectable female witness, Mrs. Whitmire, tortured the boy nigh unto death.

"This lady makes the statement that she saw them, (Bob and Print Olive) take the boy into their pasture and that she soon afterwards *heard three pistol shots, and the natural suspicion is that this sounded the death knell of this poor boy. Some months after, when the summer had set in, and the streams and water holes had dried up, a citizen discovered the skeleton of the boy in Olive's dried-up tank (pond). Finally a party determined to visit the spot and see for themselves. They went, but the demons had heard of the discovery of the bones and had removed them.*

"The bare recital of these bloody deeds throw a chill of horror over us. Yet, I. P. Olive cries up from his prison bars that he is an "innocent man" and can "establish a good character by the testimony of the best citizens in Williamson County, Texas!"

Signed: Many Citizens, Taylorsville, Texas

The editor of the <u>Platte Valley Independent</u> vented his wrath on a jury that would render such a verdict. He felt the men should have been hanged.

CHAPTER TEN

Justice is Served

Now that the Olive trial was over, Judge Gaslin could return to his interrupted regular circuit. First to be tried was Richards accused of murdering a mother and her children, and of killing one Peter Anderson - the trial to be held in Minden since the crimes were committed in Kearney County.

This was the Richards who earlier "enjoyed" the fast ride with Maggie Anderson, wife of Sheriff Anderson of Buffalo County. Gaslin had him kept in the state penitentiary for safekeeping and to prevent a mob from executing its own justice. Sheriff Anderson's wife, Maggie, in that wild buggy ride east of Kearney had foiled a mob's previous attempt. On April 26, after a quick trial the jury quickly returned a verdict of guilty in the first degree and the judge sentenced him to be hung by the neck until dead. Judge Gaslin ordered Richards returned that night to Lincoln to save him from the angry mob milling outside, which threatened to break open the jail and hang him. The judge ordered that Richards not be returned to Minden until the day of the execution.

On the appointed day of execution, at the state pen, a blacksmith was summoned to weld the bolts of the shackles placed around his ankles and handcuffs. The sheriff would see that no man tampered with these and they would have to be cut in Minden. A physician stood nearby. "Here, take this," he said, and offered him three tablespoons of brandy. To the sheriff: "Give him a shot of brandy of this size every two hours."

Richards wanted the whole bottle at once but the doctor said "no." Richards shook hands with the guards and bid them goodbye. As the grated doors swung open to let him out Print Olive and Frederick Fisher walked in.

Warden Nobes spoke to Olive and Fisher. "You can see it might have been worse for you."

"I don't know about that," replied Olive as the big door clanged shut behind them.

"I suppose you're glad to be rid of me?" Richards asked Nobes.

"No, not really," replied Nobes.

Warden Dawson, Sheriffs Kernan and Hoagland, and L. A. Kent led Richards to the carriage to take him to the rail car. As they traveled along the prisoner talked freely. "Isn't the landscape beautiful? How about picking up my mail?" The Warden had the carriage stop at the post office. There was no mail for him.

"A big crowd was waiting at the train, rushing to have a last look at the famous criminal, as though he was one of Barnam's great curiosities," said the **Lincoln Star** reporter.

When it came time to join the passengers, Sheriff Kernan held Richards' left arm and Kent his right. When he ascended the platform he asked permission to speak.

"Gentlemen, I suppose I ought to say something to you. This is my last chance to talk in public and is probably the last opportunity I shall ever have of speaking to you. I do not expect to meet any of you again in this world but hope to meet with you again hereafter. Gentlemen, I have not much to say, I give you all my best respects and hope you will all be successful in life. I now bid you good-bye."

After taking his seat in the car, he commenced smoking, said the Star. "When the cars stopped at the railroad crossing just south of the city, the cigar fell from his mouth to the floor. Raising his manacled hands to his face, he clasped them fiercely and groaned. 'My God, is there no hope!'"

The scaffold in Minden was well made with a drop of six feet. As usual, a large crowd gathered, farmers and spectators coming from miles around. They brought large lunches and swapped gossip as they waited for the event.

His minister, the Rev. Mr. Gee of Lincoln, accompanied him and made a weak attempt to provide evidence of reform in the man while he was at the pen. The shackles were unwelded by the local blacksmith.

"At twenty minutes past one o'clock he walked onto the scaffold with a firm tread, but when the officers bound his feet and arms, he was observed to be quaking somewhat," reported the **Red Cloud Chief.**

He made more objections to being bound in this manner

than he did to any other precautionary requirements of the law. From the time he was led from the guardhouse to the scaffold, he kept up a continual conversation.

"I killed Anderson in self defense," he said. "I killed him and dumped his body in the river to stop his mouth. I should not have been tried for that."

He made no excuse for killing the Harrolson family. He said he hoped "my sisters, who live outside the country, would not hear of my ignominious death. I have killed two other persons besides the Harrolson family but I killed one of them in self defense."

As the black cap was drawn over his face, he told the multitude a kind of good-bye and hoped to "meet all in another world. Now join me in singing a hymn." He selected "Come thou fount of every blessing" and all "joined in with gusto."

Reported the **Red Cloud** Chief, "Five minutes after a drop of six feet which dislocated his neck, his pulse indicated 40 beats to the minute; after ten minutes life was entirely extinct...a fine subject for contempt and a warning to all."

Assured justice was finally done, William Gaslin returned to his home in Kearney.

The Olives accused Judge Gaslin of using the famous trial as a stepping-stone to the Nebraska Supreme Court bench. Certainly the suggestion was kicked around among people of influence. The Platte Valley Independent thought it a great idea and said so in its August 23, 1879 issue:

> "The gentleman whose name leads this article is being favorably mentioned by many in our exchanges as a candidate for Supreme Court Judge. Gaslin says he is not a candidate for that position but is a candidate for the Fifth District Judgeship only.
>
> "We are for Judge Gaslin for the Supreme Court against all comers. If there were a chance to secure his nomination we believe the people of the state would secure the services of one among its most prominent jurist's, one who would have an eye for the best interest of her citizens. He would save the state tens of thousands of dollars annually by firmly refusing to grant new trials to condemned criminals on the slightest possible grounds.
>
> "The people of Buffalo County have not forgotten what the Supreme Court did for them in piling up some $15,000 in debt by granting a new trial for Jordon P. Smith, as cold blooded a murderer as ever went unhung and if there is a desire on the part

> of the people of the state to put a stop to this foolishness, no better commencement could be made than with Judge Gaslin. And while he does not seek the office, and he positively declines to enter into the fight, we are satisfied that if the Republican State Convention called upon him to be their standard bearer this fall, he would not feel himself at liberty to decline."

The judge scoffed at the idea and said he would rather just be district judge.

The battle for the open range continued in one way or another. Getting control was needed as revealed in a story in the **Bloomington Guard.** Gaslin read it with interest as he passed through on his circuit and wondered if they would have more participants in range wars.

> There was a long, strong, hard fight by cattle owners on the plains for possession of large tracts of land for grazing purposes but, so far as we can learn, they have not succeeded to any considerable extent.
>
> The homesteaders are pushing westward and are intruding upon the self-constituted sacred rights of princely cattle owners and they are considerably troubled on the state of affairs they are beginning to be crowded into. There is another great drawback to the care of large herds upon western plains. Usually the cattle will winter over with little or no care, but once in a while an unusually severe winter sets in and the poor brutes, for lack of shelter, die by the thousands.
>
> This is a country well adapted to stock raising as these vast herds have fully demonstrated, and we cannot see why the homesteader with better grade cattle and the usual care bestowed upon them, cannot make a vast improvement upon the loose style heretofore employed with good success by the heavy herders.
>
> In due course of time, when, the country becomes more fully cultivated, everything, including livestock, will settle down into better-defined channels with which people will become more fully acquainted. They will be able to make something like accurate calculation as to what can be realized from a given number of head and the ground upon which they are to feed.

CHAPTER ELEVEN

Doc Middleton – A Notorious Outlaw or a Hopeless Romantic?

Doc Middleton had a dubious beginning as a young lad growing up in Texas. Dubious because he wasn't even sure whom his father was. His father may have been James B. Riley or maybe John Shepard. He also had a favorite "uncle" whose name was Middleton, who may have been just a family friend. His mother had had three children before marrying James B. Riley. Doc Middleton grew up with the name James M. Riley, the "M" standing for Middleton. It is speculated that he acquired the name of "Doc" after helping a fellow cattle driver who had broken his leg. But most believed the nickname was the result of his being a self-educated and a fairly good horse doctor.

In addition to his unknown ancestry, Doc Middleton grew up in very poor circumstances and that may have been the cause, as a very young man, for incurring many misdemeanors and felonies before departing for safe haven in Nebraska. Before leaving Texas, he had been accused of stealing horses and jumping bail. There were also legends of three murders, one for which he served some time in prison before escaping his confines and moving on with his life, a start-over life in Nebraska.

During this time, he married for the first time. His wife was Mary E. Edwards, whom he affectionately called Lizzy. He had two sons by this marriage, however the first-born died soon after birth. The second was born while he was in jail. After he escaped from jail and was on the lam, he wrote home with the following letter:

"Grayson county texas Denison City po June the 25 1873
Dear father I seat myself to ancer your kind letter which come to hand today I was glad to her from you all an to her that you all was well this leaves me well an I hope that when the few lines comes to hand they may find you all well

and dong well I am glad to her that John is in texas I want you to rite to brother John to rite to me I would be glad to see you all I want you tell brother John to come an see me I was glad to her from lizzy and the baby I would gaive ever thng to see them but tis so that I cant it does nearly brack my hart to think about them I hant got nary leter from har cents I left thar I want you to rite to har as soon as you get this leter tell har to tak good car of har self the baby and tell har to rite to you an sister Margriet rite to me about har I want you to rite to me soon an often I am in a heap of truble about you all it is hard to think that I am a way alone so far a way from home tell mother and all of the chrilden houdy for me tell them all to rite to me so nothen mor at present so good by for a while I remaine your sun untell deth margret I hav rote to you sevler leters an I hant go neary one from you yet you musent think so hard of me for this you must excuse my bad hand rite on short leter James Riley to J.B. Riley and M. A. Riley"

Does this letter speak of his true nature, his desire to have a normal life? Not a life of crime? Some would say so. Even though he continued with a reputation of being a bad hombre, there were those who spoke of him kindly, as one who helped farmers and ranchers who were having difficult times.

Right after the Civil War, Doc's younger brother John had been a trail rider. This may have been an influence on James' decision to flee into Nebraska and become a trail rider himself. Trailing cattle from Texas to the north to be shipped to the east, on the new railroad had become a lucrative way to make a living. Cattle sold for as little as $2 a head in Texas, but if the cattle could be shipped to the east it was possible to sell them for as much as $40 a head. The costs of shipping (including the drives to the north) were $19 per head.

As this was an appealing way to make a living and because he wanted to start a new life, Middleton followed a drive into Nebraska and met up and hired on with a "freighter" operation near Sidney, Nebraska that was carrying supplies to the gold mines in South Dakota. It was here that he changed his name to Harrington (as he often did whenever he got into trouble) after the shooting of the soldier in the saloon.[*]

In spite of himself, he continued to find himself in trouble with the law or being accused of some dastardly deed. After the saloon incident and his killing of the drunken soldier in Sidney and his escape to the Black Hills of South Dakota, he started stealing horses from the Indians and ranches. He hooked up with other outlaws and became the well-known leader of the bunch. Neither the Indians nor the early settlers liked seeing the most precious tool of their trade stolen, thus the need for lawmen to seek him out or, worse yet, vigilantes ready to stretch his neck.

In spite of it all, he is lucky as noted in a biography of Middleton by Harold Hutton called "**The Luckiest Outlaw**." Middleton always seemed to slip the grasp of a lawman or a noose. After the incident in Sidney, Middleton spent more time in the north central part of Nebraska near the Niobrara River. It was here that his life took a turn with the potential for a better life. The story, as reported in the **Omaha World Herald** of June 28, 1879, was as follows:

> "Sometime since, Middleton became enamored of the daughter of a ranchman in the region through which the outlaw raided, and the girl would have been less than woman if she had not returned his affection. He reveled in his passion, proposed marriage, and was accepted.
>
> "Then came the question of where the marriage should take place and by whom the ceremony performed. There were no county officials in the neighborhood to grant the license, and no clergyman to perform the ceremony. With about twenty detectives on the lookout at the several points where these incidents of civilization could be found, this seemed by no means an easy task. He hurried off to Holt County and without trouble procured a license. Returning with two ponies and this formidable document to the abode of his charmer, the loving couple started together for the Niobrara where a clergyman was found to perform the necessary offices."

Middleton was a charmer and easily attractive to women. But this time he really fell into the proverbial love trap when he met

---

[*] See story on bottom of page 23

Mary Richardson. He proved to be a gentleman of his time by asking his future father-in-law for her hand in marriage. Her father said flatly, "No"! So they eloped! Not an easy thing for a couple to do when the law is hot on his trail.

However, the desire of Middleton was to change his life, besides his Mary wanted to see her family so he agreed to talk with her father again and one can only assume that with all his charm and courage of his convictions, Mary's father let them move back home with them.

The <u>Daily Press and Dakotan</u> of Yankton, South Dakota, August 1, 1879 reported:

> *"Middleton has lived in the Niobrara valley since last fall and during his residence there, no crime has been charged against him. He is a fine looking man, six feet in height, well proportioned, and with a frank and manly countenance.*
> *A gang of desperate thieves and outlaws infest the upper Niobrara region, but it is claimed that Middleton has no connection with them."*

It was during this time that the U.S. District Attorney and the Department of Justice hired William H.H. Llewellyn of Omaha to bring witness and bring to justice the famous outlaw. Also during this time Llewellyn met up with L. P. Hazen who had known Middleton and it was decided that they would lay a plot to entrap Middleton.

Their plan was to offer Middleton a "pardon". According to Hutton in his book, **The Notorious Outlaw,** he states, "Hazen came along to make the introduction and Llewellyn represented himself as being an emissary of the governor, with the authority to negotiate the terms for granting a pardon to Middleton. Doc had long wished for some assurance of immunity for the killing of the soldier at Sidney, since this was the only charge against him in the State of Nebraska at the time… In return for the pardon, Middleton was to give up the old life and lend his assistance to eradicating outlawry in the Niobrara-Elkhorn valley. Hazen's presence seemed to attest to the authenticity of the offer. …"

Llewellyn and Hazen then supposedly were to meet with the governor to obtain the pardon and they would return with the agreement.

Middleton was suspicious and wanted to move on (Mary was ready to leave with him), but Doc half believed that he was to have a pardon and a place on the detective force.
    When they did return, a detective also accompanied them from Wyoming by the name of William Lykens, who had had a previous skirmish with Middleton.

CHAPTER TWELVE

Doc Middleton and the Gun Battle at Long Pine

1880

Knowing that the law was after Middleton, there was no one more interested than Judge William Gaslin. By prairie telegraph and local newspapers, he and Dilworth put together quite a story of the man and his escapades. One was an account of three men who tried to capture or kill the famous outlaw.

"Those detectives, Llewellyn, Hazen and Lykens, must have been greedy for money if they thought they could get away with approaching Doc Middleton in his back yard near Long Pine," said Dilworth. "Their crude attempt is bounty hunting in the worst way."

These three, apparently, thought it was worth a try. Llewellyn had arranged with Middleton that he and Hazen would meet him at the post office in Atchison on July 18, 1880. But as Llewellyn recorded in his notes, "I expected Middleton at Atchison P.O. as per agreement. However, he did not come on account of new suspicions, and I had to employ a man to travel over to his camping place, 45 miles, to see him and carry a note to him for me." The communication back to Llewellyn was for them to meet at the Peacock's place, another post office location and supply station.

Before the three men set off to meet Middleton, Llewellyn said to Lykens, "Since you were involved in the incident at Sidney in apprehending Middleton, we don't want him to be any more suspicious than he already is. So I want you to remain hidden in the bushes along Ash Creek. We will pass by with Middleton and when I give a signal, I want you to arrest Middleton, hopefully without incident."

Llewellyn indicated in his notes that he and Hazen "rode rapidly on the main road. At 2:00 P.M., we discovered the tracks of two horses, freshly made in the road, going toward the Niobrara. We then knew that we had been closely watched.

"At 3:00 P.M., we arrived at Peacock's and were greeted by Middleton. He had with him George Holt, alias Black George,

Count Shevaloff (Bill Shelbley), and Richard Bryant alias Limber Dick, all well known Indian and government horse thieves.

"I had a long and close conversation with Middleton. At 5:00 P.M., we all took supper," stated Llewellyn.

At this point there is much confusion about what really happened as Llewellyn's reports were disguised from the truth, because he had not reported to his superiors the enticement of the fake "pardon". But according to Hutton's book, **The Luckiest Outlaw**, Llewellyn then arranged to meet Middleton with the fake pardon at Sam Liken's place, "which was about two miles upriver from Morris' crossing and out on the flat. It also appears that the three henchmen left the scene (although they were trailing behind). And when Llewellyn and Hazen met up with Middleton at Sam Liken's place, Kid Wade had joined in with the meeting and witnessed the receipt of the "pardon" from Llewellyn.

Hutton explains in his book that according to the testimonies of others,

> "Middleton and Llewellyn and party began riding downriver from Likens'. About one-and-a-half miles away Detective Lykens was concealed in the brush on the river bottom between West Laughing Water (now know as Coon Creek) and East Laughing Water. Llewellyn had to get Middleton to ride past Lykens. But how? Doc had his pardon in his pocket and all was well with the world. And it appeared now as if Middleton was going to leave the trail and head back toward the Niobrara River; this way he would not pass Lykens' hiding place. At this moment, according to Mrs. Skinner, (who testified to what she understood) the detectives brought up the matter of another paper to sign, necessitating Doc's accompanying them further. Later Llewellyn would explain that they had been going to the Skinner place to get dinner. Dinner, indeed! It was no part of Llewellyn's intention that Doc would ever see another dinner. He would ride past the thicket, there would be a blast of rifle fire, he would topple from the saddle, and the detectives would then repossess the "pardon" and tell the world that Middleton had fired first. Hazen dismounted in anticipation."

By a prearranged signal they were to race back and Hazen was to command Middleton to surrender. However, when Doc stopped watching the men after deciding there was little danger,

Hazen gave the signal. Lykens rode back and when in range, drew his revolver. But the gun stuck in his holster and fired. This spooked his horse, which promptly bucked him off. Doc fired in return but Lykens ran and hid in the brush.

Doc then aimed his gun towards Hazen. Hazen didn't go for his gun so Doc hesitated. "Pass by, Doc, and if you won't shoot, I won't either," said Hazen and repeated the offer three times. Then he said. "This whole thing has been a mistake and the matter could be satisfactorily explained."

Doc didn't buy it as his temper, was showing more and more. "I believe I could kill you."

"No you won't," yelled Hazen as he jumped off his horse, drew, and fired. Doc returned the fire and hit Hazen's horse in the shoulder. Hazen shot Doc in the abdomen. Doc's next shot hit Hazen under the left shoulder, coming out close to his backbone,

Llewellyn commenced firing but his rifle failed to fire for the first four tries. Doc and Kid Wade returned the fire and one bullet struck Llewellyn in the right hip and other places. Hazen received two balls, one in the neck and one in the arm.

All stopped firing. Kid Wade pursued Llewellyn who rode off across the prairies. Doc fell from his horse, badly wounded, he staggered off, saying to Hazen in a voice so low it was hardly understood by Hazen, "You have given me death and I have given you yours."

Hazen was too injured to answer. He staggered off in the opposite direction, falling several times. Their horses ran away.

Llewellyn came back to help Hazen, but he wasn't much help, injured as he was. "Wait until I find a horse." said Llewellyn as he staggered off. Hazen tried to follow but fell again. Finally Hazen recovered enough to make his way to a nearby homestead cabin. There the homesteader and his wife attended him. She poured whiskey into the wounds and wrapped them in strips of newly purchased muslin.

Hazen yelped with pain but her nursing stopped the bleeding. "He'll never make it. He's lost too much blood and he's so weak," said her husband.

"We did what we could," replied his wife as they stretched Hazen on the only bed in the house.

"My partners are out there and one of them is shot bad," murmured Hazen weakly.

The husband searched for Llewellyn but never found him. He did find Doc at the Werner Ranch, badly wounded. The slug had penetrated about an inch to the right of his navel. It was a glancing shot and the bullet came out about his right hip.

"Llewellyn was wounded all right. If I could walk I would go back and finish Hazen." moaned Doc.

The next morning ten of Middleton's men came hunting for Hazen. But the undaunted homesteader met them at the door with his Winchester and refused to let them in. "The first one to dismount is a dead man." he warned. His wife stood beside him with Hazen's guns in hand. None of the men wanted to make the next move. Finally they swung their horses about and rode away. "We'll get him as soon as Doc is well," promised one as they rode away.

Lykens made his way to Long Pine and ran into a posse of 20 soldiers. "How about going back with me to find Hazen and Llewellyn?" he asked, after describing the gun battle on Long Pine Creek.

They left with Lykens and found Hazen at the cabin, badly in need of medical attention.

"Let us take your wagon and haul him to Columbus where he can take a train to Omaha?" asked Lykens. "It's the only hope he has and it's a slim one."

Hazen considered Llewellyn dead. "The last I saw of him he was staggering toward the creek for a drink of water. His horse had been shot from under him and I think he will die, if not already dead. He stuck with me throughout the battle and I hope he is recovering somewhere."

The soldiers went back to find Llewellyn but never did. "I don't think he's as badly hurt as you think and he may have escaped Doc's men," said the captain.

Monday, under cover of darkness, the soldiers took Hazen to Columbus with the soldiers as guard, arriving early in the morning. The doctor there pronounced him in bad condition and said he "would be lucky to survive his wounds."

After Hazen was taken to Columbus, the homesteader went to look for Llewellyn again. But, instead, he found Doc Middleton at the Werner Ranch still in bad shape and angry. He had 40-armed men around him. "If I could, I would go to Columbus and finish off Hazen. Llewellyn got away all right. At least my men can't find him, if they do, they will finish him off too."

Doc kept on talking with difficult breath. "I may have to give up soon, but I will sell my life very dearly if they attempt to take me."

Lykens and the 20 soldiers went in quest of Middleton. However, seeing Middleton guarded by 40 of his best men, they decided now was not the time.

Doc Middleton recovered from his wounds rather quickly. He decided it was getting too hot for him in Nebraska, so he moved from Long Pine to Wyoming to where he went into horse thievery wholesale. He thought if he could get his operation out of Judge Gaslin's judicial district he would be safe.

"Maybe the reason he thought the show was about over in Nebraska was the lynching of Kid Wade in Long Pine by vigilantes," offered Dilworth.

Posters continued to appear in western Nebraska offering a reward for Doc Middleton's arrest "dead or alive" and the reward was often raised as new posters appeared. Big cattlemen were angry and frustrated over his horse thievery. They were more determined than ever to "stretch his neck".

Middleton would gather horses from herds in Western Nebraska or eastern Wyoming, hurry them east and sell to farmers and ranchers outside the brand inspection areas.

The judge read each poster he ran across with renewed interest.

"Looks as if we'll get him in court yet if they don't get him first," he told Dilworth.

As reported by S.D Butcher (early day Nebraska photographer and historian), Llewellyn, after recovery from wounds inflicted by Doc Middleton in a gun battle south of Long Pine, rode to Ft. Hartsuff, twenty five miles south, where he got together a squad of soldiers under Happy Jack, a United States scout. Happy Jack soon located Middleton who surrendered. Lykens, now a marshal from Wyoming, insisted Middleton stand trial for horse stealing in Wyoming. There he was convicted but since Wyoming's prison had been damaged in a fire, Middleton was sent to Nebraska to serve his five years prison sentence.

Knowing the cattlemen's temper and the possibility they would take him themselves, Judge Gaslin ordered Deputy Warden Nobes from the state prison to pick him up.

Nobes arrived in Cheyenne and took Middleton under his control. When the train stopped in Sidney, Nobes had Middleton take an upper birth. "And be very quiet" said Nobes. "We might have company yet."

Before the train could start, four men, one of them being a "heavy" stockman of the county, entered the coach with more than normal self-confidence. He stepped back when he saw Nobes. "Hello!" said the cattleman.

"You here? I thought Doc was coming down with the sheriff of Cheyenne County?"

Nobes jumped up. "Yes, I am here, and I want you to leave this car immediately."

The leader hesitated, but for only a moment. "We have come after Middleton, and we're going to have him. We have a party outside fully able to take care of him, and it will not cost the State a cent to keep him any longer."

Nobes arose and, with a revolver in each hand, ordered the men "to leave this car at once!" They left.

As soon as the train moved on, Nobes called Middleton from the berth. He asked the conductor where he could hide his prisoner until after the next station was passed. He offered the directors' car, the last on the train. Doc was hurried into the car, the doors locked, windows closed and the lights extinguished.

Upon arrival at the next station, Chappell, the train was boarded by a large number of armed men who walked through the cars scanning everybody closely. Failing to find their man they asked the trainmen if Warden Nobes and Middleton were on the train. The conductor answered "no," that they had gotten off the train at Sidney. Satisfied with this answer, they left and returned to Sidney.

A reporter from the **Lincoln Journal** described Middleton's entry into Lincoln:

> *Doc Middleton, the noted outlaw and desperado, who has been the terror of stockmen in the northwestern part of the state for the past years, arrived on Monday's train from the west in charge of Deputy Warden Nobes and taken to the pen to undergo a sentence of*

five years. In appearance he is not what we expected to see. He is neither a large or small man and his physique doesn't indicate great strength. Taken altogether, he is a rather good-looking man. He has very high cheekbones, piercing black eyes and a mouth to indicate great firmness.

He was seated in the waiting room of the depot for fifteen minutes after the arrival of the train conversing with a stranger and, to look at him, not knowing who he is; he would be the last person in the room taken for an outlaw or desperado. When the carriage, which was to take him to the pen, was ready he arose from his seat and walked to it quickly, as though anxious to get to his new home.

The carriage passed up "O" Street to Eleventh, when it turned and went south. Middleton was seated in the back seat and his restless eyes seemed to take in everything as he moved along.

Our informant is confident that if the last gang (at Chappell) could have laid hands on Middleton that night, he would now be in the home of his forefathers.

His new wife, Mary wrote the following in a long letter July 29,1979 to Doc's mother:

"Mrs. Riley

Dear friend....He has a wife that will stick to him as long as he livs no matter what his fate is I knew him well before we was married and I will stay close to him in all truble never one has his truble sooner ore latter Jack sends his love all best respects to you all and to the girls he ways if he lives and lucks well he will come and see you all..."

Middleton did live, but she did not live up to her word. It is speculated that she got tired of waiting for him to get out of prison. Besides her father was still working on her to change her life. She did.

When Middleton did get out of jail, he returned for Mary, but found her unavailable. Much to the chagrin of Mary's father, Middleton took up with his youngest daughter, Rene. And they seemingly had a happy life. Doc really never did return to his old ways again. And Judge Gaslin never did get his day in court with him.

CHAPTER THIRTEEN

Appeals Court – an Outrageous Decision

1880

Every day Print Olive and Frederick Fisher were sent out to break rocks. Every night they came back to their cells to nurse blistered hands and sore muscles. And every night Print cursed Judge Gaslin, District Attorney Dilworth, the jury and everyone involved in the trial that took away his liberty. He understood why some men convicted for murder sometimes asked to be hung rather than go to the state prison.

Olive and Fisher had been incarcerated for most of a year now. But anyone who thought Olive was going to rot in the pen and spend the rest of his life pounding rocks, hadn't reckoned with a man who had shot his way through troubles all the way from Texas and, with his brothers Ira and Bob, built a herd of 15,000 cattle and 4,000 horses. He was too used to doing what he wanted and removing obstacles as they arrived. He had been used to beginning every day with getting on a horse to go out to brand and sort his herds and send the surplus to market. To be confined to a jail cell at night and work on a rock pile in the day was just too much for a man who had spent his life in the outdoors.

He called in his attorneys Hinman, Neville, Mason, Whedon, James Laird, Hamer and Conner. Laird answered his call. Laird was also a member of the state legislature.

"When are you getting me out of this hell hole?" stormed Olive. "This is driving me crazy."

"We're working on it," said Laird. Olive knew that the case had been appealed to the Nebraska Supreme Court on several grounds, most importantly on the issue of the change of venue in holding the trial in Hastings where Olive and Fisher were convicted.

An act passed by the state legislature February 24, 1879, divided Custer County between two judicial districts. It went into effect one day before the famous trial began. Laird argued before the Nebraska Supreme Court that this nullified the trial.

Whether Laird pressured the state legislature to pass this act before the trial began is not known but, most assuredly, he was suspected of doing so. It certainly had the desired effect as far as two members of the Nebraska Supreme Court were concerned. They used it to nullify the conviction and move it back to the new county of Custer for a new trial.

A statute passed by the state legislature in February 25, 1875, authorized district court judges to "designate the county where an indictment may be found if the crime is committed in an unorganized county." Judge Gaslin used the strength of this statute to move the trial to Adams County and to select jurors from anywhere in his district.

True, Custer County was an organized county by this time being organized in 1877. But in the process of dividing the wide-ranging District Five into two districts a peculiar thing happened; Custer County was divided with the south half in District Five and the north half in District Six. No one came forth with a satisfactory explanation for this but it may have had something to do with the fact that the county was so large that many assumed it would be divided into two or more counties eventually. In fact there were efforts made to divide it further.

Moreover, it was unconstitutional, both state and national, to divide a county into portions of two districts.

This meant, in effect, that Custer County was in no judicial district at all. Because of this aberration, Gaslin, using the 1875 statute, felt justified in moving the trial outside of Custer County where the crime had been committed.

The latest act (1879) ordered trials to be held in the county where the crime was committed and jurors to be selected from residents of that county. The Nebraska Supreme Court, in a two-to-one decision, said the latest act repealed the act of 1875 with no grandfather clause allowing for trials to be held elsewhere in the interim.

Justices George B. Lake and Amasas Cobb of the Nebraska Supreme Court argued to nullify the Olive conviction based on the above facts and the latest statute.

A majority of the Supreme Court argued, "We have no hesitation in deciding that the district court in Adams County was without jurisdiction, and that the entire proceedings resulting in the conviction and sentence of the prisoners are erroneous for that reason..."

Chief Justice Samuel Maxwell dissented. "I cannot give my assent. It may be conceded that a district for the trial of a person accused of crime cannot be formed after the commission of the alleged offense. And in my opinion that has not been done in this case." Judge Maxwell, in effect, argued that a crime had been committed and the perpetrators of the crime must be tried somewhere and that Judge Gaslin had done what was necessary to promote justice.

Gaslin said, "Judge Samuel Maxwell, all honor to him, dissented in one of the ablest legal documents ever prepared in that court."

Although the Nebraska Supreme Court (at least two of them) disapproved of Judge Gaslin's handling of the attorneys (like fining Laird), the jurors and the witnesses in the Olive matter. In the end, it was the location of the trial which produced the reversal of Olive's conviction. In short, he got a new trial because of a technicality. The statute, which allowed Gaslin to conduct the trial in Hastings, was declared unconstitutional. It may never be known whether the decision was the result of brilliant legalese or Olive-inspired legislation, but the result was the same: Print Olive got a new trial, this time in the friendly confines of Custer County.

The prisoners were returned to Custer County and tried before County Judge Boblits in Custer City. There were no witnesses and no complaint on the docket and so the judge said, "Since there are no witnesses to the case and no trial attorneys, the case is dismissed." He scribbled a few notes in his account book among notations about purchases of salt and other mundane things, thus conducting one of the shortest trials, we believe, in all Nebraska history.

Ex-Senator Thurston stated: "The Supreme Court rendered what seems to me and still seems to me to be the most outrageous decision that I have ever known."

Carl Smith, noted Custer County historian, said in his book, **History of Custer County**, "The results of this decision were that, until the constitution permitted a division of judicial districts. Custer County was and would remain a sanctuary for criminals it being impossible for a man to be tried for any serious crime committed in that county ... "

This meant that Judge Gaslin could not hold a new trial for Olive and Fisher in any county in his judicial district. The decision was an obvious, and successful, attempt to tie his hands in the case. He fumed and said a few more unkind things about the Nebraska Supreme Court. He was already at odds with the Supreme Court over some of its antics. They were, no doubt, troubled over his great popularity in his district, he said.

Print Olive thanked his attorney for his help and for the results. Then he rode out to look over his vast domain to see how the cattle were doing. He found them well cared for by his father and brother, Ira, while he was in the prison.

He also licked his wounds, not bodily, but financially, which were next to disastrous. Judge Gaslin assessed him the cost of the bringing in the army for the trial in Hastings---$10,000. But that cost may have been mild when compared with the cost of an army of lawyers. But they had accomplished what he wanted most, his freedom.

But the malfunction of the system would not interfere with Gaslin's continuing with the job for which he was elected to the best of his ability. He would still lay a couple of six-shooters on the bench before a trial started. He was still the terror of criminals.

Said the Wahoo Independent:

"The widows of Mitchell and Ketchum, whose bodies were found burned and charred where they had been left by I. P. Olive and his gang, have been settled with by said Olive, he paying them $750 as a recompense for the loss of their husbands[*]. And yet this man Olive guilty of their murder almost beyond the shadow of a doubt, by means of mere legal technicalities, goes unwhipped of justice. A court that would thus free murderers is almost as guilty as the criminal himself. What a burlesque on law and what a travesty on justice."

Perhaps this compassionate act was due to the kindly qualities of Mrs. Olive. The Loup City Times reported on June 10, 1881,

---

[*] Ketchum was not married but had courted Tamar Snow, a daughter of Mrs. Mitchell by a previous marriage.

"...that Mrs. Luther Mitchell has gone to Plum Creek[*] to live, and hints that she will live upon the bounty of I. P. Olive, her husband's murderer. If assertions of persons who claim to know the family to be true, Mrs. Mitchell is quite as well off in the house of her enemies as that of her friends. The latter it is claimed sold her husband to this murderer and then, under the guise of friendship, robbed her of what little property she had left.[**] The Mitchell and Ketchum murder is a dark and bloody affair and their blood is upon the hands of others than Olive and his associates.

"Is it not about time that the people of Nebraska thought of elevating the standard of ability on their supreme court? There are certainly better lawyers in the state than any of the Supreme Court judges. At all events, if technicalities have to be substituted for law and justice as in the cases of Smith (Fisher) and Olive, let us have a court that has the ability to cover their decisions with an appearance of common sense."

---

[*] Renamed Lexington
[**] Could the writer have been alluding to her "friend," Judge Wall?

CHAPTER FOURTEEN

Judge Gaslin's Circus of Circuits

Earlier in the year, 1881, Judge William Gaslin announced court times for the ten counties in District Five:

Adams County: May 3rd, June 21st and December 9th
Buffalo County: April 20th, June 15th and November 30th
Cheyenne County: April 6th and October 26th
Dawson County: April 27th and November 23rd
Franklin County: March 26th and November 10th
Furnas County: October 5th.
Harlan County: March 30th and November 16th
Kearney County: May 25th and October 19th
Keith County: June 1st.
Lincoln County: April 13th and October 29th.
Phelps County: May 28th.
Red Willow County: October 7th.
Sherman County: October 13th.
Webster County: March 23rd, June 29th and November 4th.

Other counties in District Five included were Hitchcock, Dundy, Chase, and Frontier.[*]

"Terms of Court will be called in either or all of the other counties in the district when the commissioners thereof desire, of which due notice will be given," he wrote.

And notices they did write as the back of the criminal was not yet broken. In fact Gaslin spent most of his time riding the circus of circuits.

---

[*] *Note that Custer County is not mentioned.*

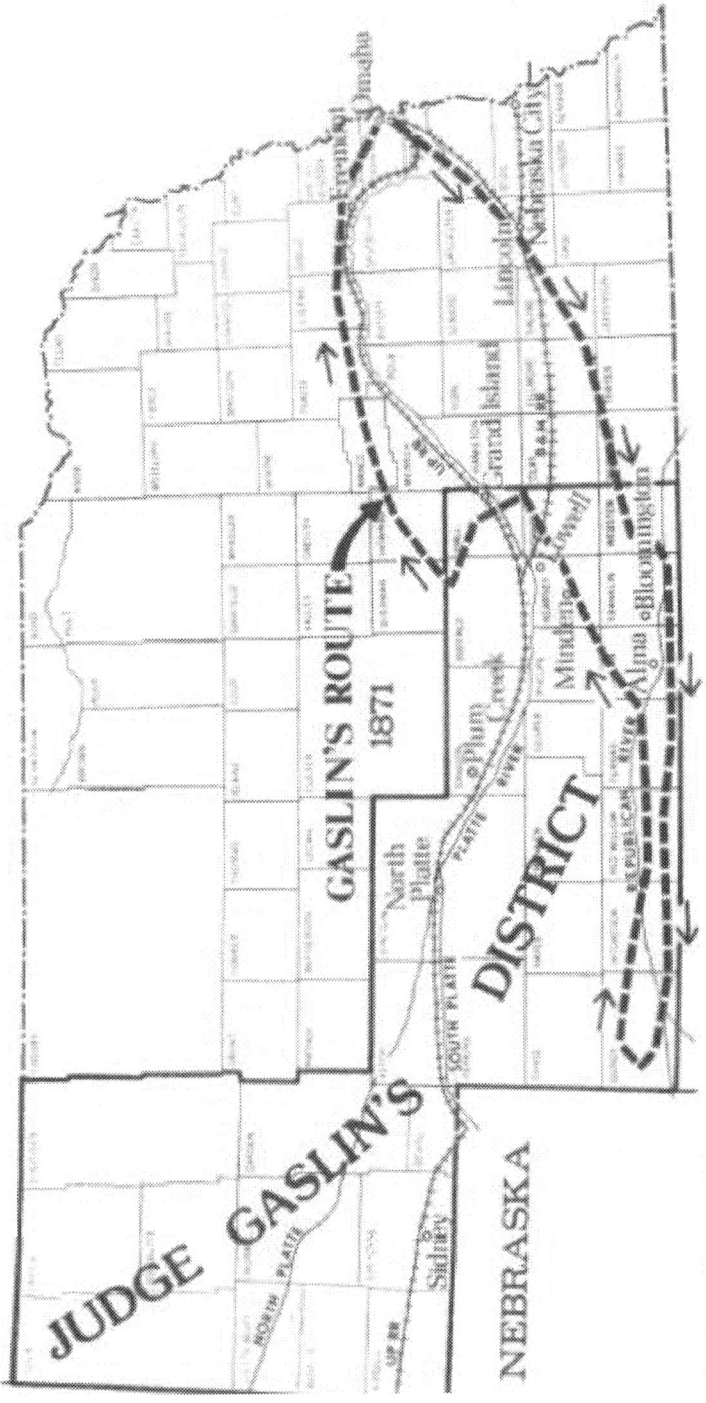

Gaslin's Trip to Western Nebraska and Star Judicial District

Frank D. White and his wife, Mary, sitting on the veranda at a hotel in Lincoln, discussed what to do - keep his job as a blacksmith or go west as many people were doing. It was mid-March, 1880. As they watched the sun approach the horizon in a blazing sunset and ceased their conversation, they saw an older man with a newly painted wagon, but one not in the best of condition. He tied his team to the hitching rail and went into the hotel dining room. The wagon was loaded with all sorts of farm equipment including a sod breaking plow and tools. A tarp covered part of the items. Mary noted the situation and it sparked a gleam in Frank's eye. "Let's go talk to him. He looks like someone heading west and he looks like a granger," suggested Frank. Inside they saw the stranger sitting at a table. Frank walked over and introduced himself, then asked if they could join him at supper, "Sure. Vy not?" answered the man in an accent that branded him of German descent. "My name is William Rozier. I'm going vest to get me a farm and grow crops."

During supper they talked of the West, the potential for riches on a homestead on the prairie. And they sized each other up. Will, a farm boy revealed he was from Iowa and confided he had some money and Frank confessed they had very little, "Maybe ve can make a deal and go out together," said Will.

They did make a deal: they would homestead on separate farms, use Rosier's money until they could harvest and sell a crop. After that they would split the profits.

Both men homesteaded ten miles west of Arapahoe. While Rosier plowed the tough sod, Frank and Mary cut sod and built a small house and barn on the White homestead. Will Rosier was out at daylight plowing sod, then in the evening when it was getting dark and the horses were tired, he came in and helped build the house and barn.

Together they planted corn for a crop and sorghum for horse feed. But by the time they got around to planting the crops the season was late and a drought had cut the prospect to less than half that they would need for a profit. And Will was running out of money.

That summer Frank White bought on credit from local stores but now they were crowding him for payment. The Whites suggested to Will that they mortgage his team to a bank but Will said "No. Ve yust have to get a job."

They argued and Frank became morose and quarrelsome. One day he drove to the bank in Cambridge, a few miles west, and mortgaged Rosier's team for $65, then drove back to an Arapahoe bank and borrowed another $25, using the same team for credit. He didn't tell Rosier what he had done but he did tell his wife.

"You can't mortgage Will's property," said Mary. "He'll be fighting mad when he hears of it."

"I'll take care of him," said Frank.

He came home June 28 with a chunk of lamb and a bottle of strychnine. Mary joined him in the plot and they poured the strychnine over the meat and fed it to Will for supper that night. Will took a bite, and then sickened. He loafed around the house for a day, and then recovered.

August 18, Frank returned home with two bottles of beer, a drink highly favored by Will. He poured the poison into the beer and offered it to Will when he came in that evening, "That vas nice of you," said Will who gulped down one bottle, grabbed his stomach and went into convulsions.

Neighbors that stopped in at the White and Rosier homestead on August 20 quickly noted that Rosier was not there. They asked about him, knowing by now the rift developing between the two men. White said Rosier had gone to Iowa to help his father with his oat harvest. This satisfied their curiosity.

Later the president of the Republican Valley Bank in Arapahoe learned that the Whites planned to leave also, driving the mortgaged team. He sent Vice President Delatour to take one of the horses, which had been mortgaged. The Furnas County Bank in Cambridge, hearing the same rumor, sent deputy sheriff Burton after them with a warrant to arrest the Whites for obtaining money under false pretenses. As they were returning with the Whites, they were met by a party from Cambridge who said they had found Rosier's body under a manure pile. Delatour and the men reported to the county attorney who called a coroner's inquest.

At the inquest, testimony of witnesses implicated the Whites. But Frank D. White testified in his own behalf. "About the 15th of March, we, my wife and I, were in Lincoln, and I had secured a job of work in a blacksmith shop. I met Rozier at the hotel and was induced by him to come west and take up a claim. He was to pay all expenses and to furnish a team, which he had. We came west, lived together in peace and friendship, we entertaining the highest respect for him. Owing to the failure of crops and hard times me and Rozier concocted a scheme to mortgage the team, which I did, both at the Bank at Cambridge for $65 and at Arapahoe for $25, and then run the team off, which I intended to do had we not been stopped and arrested. As to Rozier, he was taken to Cambridge, and was to go back to Iowa, and write to us at Lincoln where we were to join him, Lincoln being the place we were going to. "I gave him $20 and returned home that evening before dark. I believe some other party murdered Rozier and buried him there to throw suspicion on us. I am 25 years old, was born at Oran, N. Y., living there 21 years, and following my trade of blacksmithing..."

Several men discounted the statement about getting along together. One said Rozier stated, "He wanted to get away. Was afraid of White and would leave." He said Rozier was an honest old man and would never enter into a swindling scheme such as White claims.

After examining various other witnesses the grand jury returned an indictment of three counts. Frank D. White was charged with the murder of William Rozier on August 20, 1880. Mary was not charged.

The editor of the <u>Arapahoe Pioneer</u> added "the many connecting circumstances make a strong chain of evidences and if White escapes hanging by law the probabilities are he will never leave the county alive, as the feeling is intense, and all feel a firm conviction he and his wife murdered Rozier."

Judge Gaslin ordered White's trial to be held October 5, 1880 in a small building in Arapahoe. The charge stated "that a large quantity of deadly poison, called strychnine, to wit, six grains of deadly poison, called strychnine, put, mixed and mingled into and with a certain quantity of beer, to wit: one pint of beer. After Rosier drank it he became mortally sick and distempered in his body...and died."

The judge opened the trial with little fanfare. As per his custom, he laid two heavy Colt revolvers on the old desk that served as a bench, removed his coat and tie and called the court to order. The judge was not particularly worried about the spectators who packed the small room although there was plenty of talk about a lynching. There were a few gun-toting cowboys, as most were still on the fall roundup. But they had no special interest in the trial. What happened to a granger was not their worry, maybe a couple less farmers to take up land that was disappearing under the plow and reducing the cattle range and their job by that much. But there were hot tempers in the crowd, people who thought the couple should hang and they just might take the law into their own hands. The revolvers on the judge's desk suggested they not try.

Acting district attorney T. D. Scofield read the charge, accusing White of killing Rosier.

Peter B. Burgo was the first witness:

"I have been acquainted with the defendant, Frank D. White, since some time in April, 1880. White stayed at my place camping in a canyon for two weeks when he first came to the county. William Rosier came with him and lived with him on Section 6, Township 3, Range 24, in a sod house or dugout. Rosier lived with him until I saw him no more. Last saw Rosier in May when he and White were at my house.

"Next saw him dead on Frank D. White's place on September 1, 1880 at the same farm. I found him dead inside of a grave, which was about 103 feet from the house door. It was 51 feet from the northwest corner of the house to the grave and six feet from the northwest corner of the stable, and it was fourteen feet from the middle of the stable door to the grave. The grave was about three feet deep, one and one-half feet wide and five feet, six inches long. It was about 10 o'clock in the forenoon when I found him. There were several other persons there. I recognized the body to be that of William Rosier... He had on a pair of overalls and striped shirt and a pair of common shoes. His hair was rather sandy and his moustache was more grey than sandy.

"I saw White on August 29 and asked where Rosier had gone and he said he had gone to Iowa. On August 26, he told me that he and Rosier went to Cambridge and that Rosier had received a letter from friends in Iowa and that his father was sick and wanted him to come and take care of his oats, as they were rotting and he immediately took the train for Iowa, and that he had let him have $25 to go with... White promised Rosier he would take his team to him in Iowa and when he got there Rosier was to pay him back his money.

"White said he had authority to sell Rosier's property and on the August 29 I bargained for the crops of both men and he sold me Rosier's corn and hay.

Frank Albright's testimony:

"I have known the defendant and deceased since last spring. They were neighbors of mine. I last saw Rosier on August 15, Sunday, at his house. He seemed to be well and in good health then. I next saw him on September 1, dead, on Frank D. White's place, under a manure pile about 9 o'clock in the morning. There was a great crowd there. White told me on August 22 that Rosier got a letter from his father in Iowa, that his oats were lying rotting on the ground and he went right off to Iowa. White said "I took his trunk to Arapahoe yesterday."

"The third time I talked with him I asked him where Rosier was. He would not tell me; said he did not know. .."

George Sayers' testimony was:

"I have seen Frank D. White, but never the deceased until I helped take the body out of the grave under the manure pile on Frank D. White's place on Sept, 1, 1880. Went with my haying hands and helped. Al Brown, Andrews and his three boys were there."

Doctors Annise, Howard and Morgan stated that they made a postmortem examination and extracted the stomach and gave their report to the sheriff. Also said that, in their opinion, death was caused by poison.

James John, a druggist testified: "White, the defendant, bought strychnine at my store on June 28 and August 18, 1880. First time, he bought five grains, and the second time about six grains."

D. M. Tomblin, a banker stated, "I have had experience in hand-writing. I have White's signature to a note and mortgage and this is the man that signed these letters. They are the same. (Notes and letters offered in evidence.) The mortgage was made August 16, 1880, and he said it was a team he brought from Pennsylvania."

William Albright stated:

"I have known the defendant and the deceased since about April 1. I last saw Rosier August 15, 1880 at my father's house and he appeared to be in good health then. On August 16 I was with

White as we went into a saloon and where he bought three bottles of beer and put them in his wagon and drove off, saying the beer was for Rosier and that he did not like liquor. On August 22 White told me in my sod corn field that Rosier had left the country and he told me about the letter Rosier got from his father in Iowa. Rosier owned a wagon, a bay horse and a grey horse, and a breaking plow. The team was the same one that White mortgaged."

G. M. Goble said: "White stopped overnight at my place on August 30. Said he was going to Pennsylvania with the team he had with him."

John Kirtchoffer: "Last saw Rosier on August 18 or 19 at Schwap's blacksmith shop. White was with him."

Elizabeth Davis stated she "Saw Frank and Mary White go past on August 21. Said he was going to Arapahoe to take the old man's things as he had gone to Iowa."

Prof. Samuel Aughey: "Testified to receiving a human stomach in Lincoln from this county. Found traces of strychnine in it."

Judge Gaslin charged the jury as follows: "If any person shall purposely and in deliberate and premeditated malice, or in the perpetration, or attempt to perpetrate any rape, poison, or causing the same to be done, kill another... every person so offending shall be deemed guilty of murder in the first degree and upon conviction thereof shall suffer death."

But he offered two other options to the jury: "Under the indictment in this case upon the principle that the lesser crime is embraced in the greater, you may render a verdict of murder in the second degree, under section 4, General Statutes of Nebraska; which reads: "If any person shall purposely and maliciously, but without deliberation and premeditation, kill another, every such person shall be deemed guilty in the second degree, and upon conviction thereof, shall be imprisoned in the penitentiary not less than ten years, or during life, in the discretion of the court.

"If you find there is no positive evidence in the case, consequently you will bear in mind that all the circumstances proved must form one connected chain, from which no link can be spared or wanting, and which can be explained upon no other reasonable hypothesis than the guilt of the accused; and should you find the facts and circumstances proved in this case be accounted for upon other reasonable hypothesis than the guilt of the defendant, it is your duty to acquit him."

The jury pronounced Frank D. White guilty in the second degree and Judge Gaslin, on October 15, sentenced him to life imprisonment at hard labor.

In other court action this term in Arapahoe, the case of L. D. Carroll, accused and indicted for cattle stealing, was carried over until the next term of court. The prisoner was released on his own recognizance.

Dudly Merrill and Cynthia Wilkenson were indicted by the grand jury for fornication, but settled the matter by the district attorney entering "nolle prosequi" (unwilling to pursue) and "the sweet pair were united by the holy bonds of wedlock."

Dick Belmont and Mart Zimmerman, fresh off a roundup and living up their hard-earned money in the saloons of Minden, walked into the restaurant and started harassing the waitresses. One of the waitresses sent word to Sheriff Jack Woods who came immediately.

"You men are under arrest," he said sternly as he entered the cafe.

Belmont whipped out his six-shooter and shot the sheriff dead. His partner and he mounted their horses and rode south out of town as fast as their mounts could carry them.

A posse, gotten together quickly, took after them. They were sure they were headed for Kansas. They lost the trail in northwest Kansas, a thinly settled territory. Another posse, led by Adjutant General S. Alexander, went after them from the McCook area in an effort to head them off from that direction.

Belmont and Zimmerman rode south into Furnas County until their horses gave out. Then four miles northwest of Lyndon Hills they stole two good horses and left their exhausted ones and rode hard southwest. On Oct. 18, they were seen about twenty miles northeast of the divide between Sappa Creek and Beaver Creek. The next day they were seen riding southwest in Kansas, around Lenora.

Alexander and a large group headed southwest of Lenora, hoping to intercept the outlaws before they got into Oklahoma. Nebraska Governor Nance received a telegram from the constable of Lenora stating that two men, brothers of the murderers, had been arrested at that place Thursday night on a charge of horse stealing.

At Buffalo Park, formerly Buffalo Gap, forty miles southwest of Lenora, Alexander split his men into small groups and began scouring the whole area of western Kansas, The hunted men were seen by a settler crossing the north fork of the Solomon River. Sheriff Wilboro of Abilene left with a posse from that region to try to cut them off from that way.

The men were surrounded in November near Lakin, in Kearny County, Kansas, and in the shootout, Belmont was killed and Zimmerman, Kelley and Collins were captured.

The <u>Custer County Republican</u>, dated Nov. 9, 1882, stated, "that the desperado who killed the Kearney County sheriff has been killed and can no longer murder honest men and steal horses. Kelly and Collins, part of the same gang, are under arrest and are being returned to Nebraska to answer for their crimes."

Judge Gaslin did not set their trial dates nor would they be until he could fit them into his busy circuit.

Gun slinging outlaws and their henchmen had one thing in common: They died young and usually a violent death, either by hanging or by being shot, sometimes by each other as in the case of Jesse James who was shot by a friend in exchange for clemency. At best they were serving long terms in a state prison and most thought death a preferred alternative to the prison. Long hours on a rock pile breaking the rock into small pieces was not something to look forward to. They knew they would receive rough treatment by prison guards. Guns and tough judges such as William Gaslin were making life rough for the criminals.

"They that live by the sword shall die by the sword, says the Bible," commented Dilworth during a long train trip up the Republican Valley.

The <u>Red Cloud Chief</u> of June 29, 1882, stated:

"As illustrative of the oft made statement that those who prey upon society become victims of society."

The following from the <u>Indianapolis Sentinel</u>:

> *"It is by no means uninteresting to read the fate of the members of the James gang of outlaws who, for a number of years pasts have made it exceedingly dangerous to travel west of*

the Mississippi River or to conduct a banking business anywhere in the far west outside large cities. We have the record of twenty-nine members of the gang, coming down to the killing of Jesse James, (by one of his so called friends for the reward and clemency).

Hite ....killed
Jeff Hite .... 25 years in the pen.
John Younger...killed
Bud Younger .... killed
Tom McDaniels..killed
Billy Barry......killed
Joe Collins......killed
Bill Heflren...killed
Arkansas Johnson..killed
Sam Bass .... killed (In Texas by Texas Ranger in a gun battle. He was never tried for a train robbery)
Harry Collins..killed
Billy Collins...killed
Bill Caldwell..killed
Charlie Pitt .... killed
Cid Miller .... killed
Jesse James .... killed

In penitentiaries: Pipes, 99 years, Herndon, 99 years, Jack Keene, 34 years, Tucker, 25 years, Bashan, 25 years, Billy Ryan, 25 years. Frank James wounded. (He reformed and lived out his natural life.)

"Four are on trial and will be sent to prison or to the scaffold. Only one of the gang so far, Arthur McCoy, has died a natural death," said the editor.

Judge Gaslin sent his share of the men either to the gallows or the pen. Most of the big names in crime had already ended their career one way or another.

CHAPTER FIFTEEN

LAW OF A DIFFERENT KIND

At the St. Louis boarding house in Hastings, James Green, Fred Ingraham and John Babcock sat eating a late supper. Green pulled the colored table cover from the table where they sat drinking coffee after the meal was eaten and tucked it under his coat. The waiter suggested it was time to close and the men left. Back in their room Green and Ingraham discussed whom they could rob and pick up some money, money to replace what they had lost at the previous night's poker game at a saloon. They decided on Millett, a storekeeper who closed late and often worked late. Babcock, a young man who had fallen into company with the other two, was not so enthused about robbing anyone. "Let's just stick to diggin' wells," he said. The three had been hired to dig a water well for Charles Kohl south of town.

"This is a lot easier," pointed out Green, "we've been doing this for a long time and no problems. We're too smart to get caught. The police are afraid of us.

Millett finished his bookwork, grabbed his moneybag, and left for home, walking west. He had gone no more than two blocks when, at First and Bellevue, three men stepped out and ordered him to go with them.

"Give me that bag and keep walking until we arrive at that cave west of the city limits," Green ordered him.

Millett held back and the men prodded him to hurry. When they reached the Aaron May residence he broke away from them and ran to the house, hoping to reach the door and run inside. As he ran, Green fired. Millett was hit but reached the back door of the May home and knocked. When Mrs. May opened the door he fell into her arms, blood from his wounds staining her nightgown. She saw the men run down the street toward the boarding house.

Millett was taken inside and laid on a bed and a doctor summoned. Early that morning he made a statement to Dr. Isaac Le Doyt about the identity of the men but he was rather incoherent. Then he died. Aaron May notified Sheriff Joe Williams.

One of the men dropped the tablecloth as they ran, which

later served as evidence. The sheriff picked it up and it was identified as taken from the boarding house table. But this was the only clue.

The waiter who served the men the night before identified the cloth and observed that the cloth was missing after the men left.

That was enough evidence for the sheriff. They found the men digging a well for Kohl and arrested them. People were so angry over this needless slaying they talked of a lynching. The county judge ordered the prisoners taken to Lincoln for safe keeping until the trial.

Judge Gaslin directed district attorney James Dilworth to prepare for a preliminary hearing on April 28, 1882. They rode the train to Hastings for the trial and stayed at one of the hotels. The men were returned from Lincoln on a train the same date. Gaslin ordered a heavy guard placed around the prisoners, expecting an effort at mob lynching.

That night, at a dance at Liberal Hall, still the Adams County courthouse, Charles H. Deitrich, who was state senator and was later to become governor of Nebraska, overheard talk of lynching. He was not sure of the guilt of all the men.

He hastily left the hall, talked with Gaslin at his room, and secured permission to speak with Babcock, "I don't think he was a willing party to the crime and he might talk," explained Deitrich.

Babcock, a lad of 18, confessed to Deitrich verbally and in writing. "I'll see what I can do to save your life in return for this," Dietrich told him. "I'd sure appreciate that," said the nervous Babcock. That night thirty-three men met at the lumberyard on the south side of the tracks. They all came in masks and moved with the precision of trained soldiers to where the prisoners were being kept in the Stone Block under heavy guard. The "Committee of 33", as they came to be called, overpowered the guards and proceeded to batter down the doors.

They seized the three men and took them north along the St. Joseph and Grand Island RR track and there proceeded with the work of lynching, Dietrich and a crowd of men and a few women accompanied the committee, Dietrich demanding that Babcock be spared. The committee refused to listen. The ropes were placed about the necks of the three men. Twice Dietrich broke through the line and threw the rope from Babcock's neck. But the committee forced him back and strung Babcock up along with the other two. Again, Deitrich broke through and this time severed Babcock's rope. His determination finally won him a hearing.

Dietrich made a speech on behalf of Babcock. "I promised Babcock his life in return for a confession and, by God, I'll keep that promise or die with him," he shouted.

Babcock was spared. The two men were pushed from the bridge. Ingraham's neck was broken with the fall; Green choked to death. Neither would confess before the committee although given a chance.

Judge Gaslin knew nothing of the incident until morning, having gone to bed instead of to the dance. He walked to the scene. Walking around the swaying body of Ingraham and the body of Green on the ground (The morning train cut his rope) he turned to the crowd and said:

"Well, there is one verdict the damned Supreme Court won't reverse."

Because of his impatience with legal technicalities and incidents, and his penchant for directness, the Supreme Court overruled many of his decisions.

Babcock was tried later and sentenced to 10 years in prison for manslaughter. After seven years he was pardoned and he disappeared.

Sometimes men thought they would settle their own problems instead of letting Judge Gaslin settle them. And, often, the matter was a over a farmer's field or a rancher's livestock, in this case Ira Olive's horses and a farmer's corn field.

Two of Ira's cowboys, W. H. Stewart and S. Hagadone, were taking horses across country to good winter range. Schryer, a farmer and a man named Nelson had an unfenced cornfield. The cowboys either didn't want to go around it or the fractious horses sped across the field, knocking down corn and eating some.

It was a sorry looking field after they crossed and the new homesteaders were mad. A few days later they spotted some of Olive's horses in a draw and shot them. Those same cowboys, Stewart and Hagadone, finding the dead animals, decided to investigate.

But, first, they stopped in Custer City and filled up on whiskey. Then they stopped at the Schryer sod house and there ran into Nelson and another farmer by the name of Bainbridge, the latter having had a few words with Stewart previously. Bainbridge threatened the men. "Get out!"

The two boys drew their revolvers and backed out of the house, just as they came out of the house Schryer came around the corner of the house.

"Put that gun down!" yelled Schryer and grabbed Stewart's wrist.

"Let go of my gun!" bellowed Stewart.

As they struggled over the gun it fired, going through Stewart's right hand and entering Schryer's breast. The cowboys jumped on their horses and raced south.

Bainbridge and Nelson carried Schryer in the house, laid him on a bed, and rode hard to Custer City for Dr. Brisbain. The doctor found the ball under Schryer's right side. It had probably followed a rib bone around and lodged there, said the doctor.

Constable Morgan of Delight rode to Plum Creek[*] to see the sheriff and try to head off the men. The cowboys, he learned, had boarded a westbound passenger train. A few telegrams revealed they had left the train and were nowhere to be found. The sheriff posted a $100 reward for their arrest. The men were never located.

"The crime was committed in Custer County," commented Gaslin, "and could not be prosecuted anyway."

<u>McCook Weekly</u>, Dec. 20, 1883 –

> Information was received on the 12th from the Niobrara Valley to the effect that a vigilante committee has made war with five horse and cattle thieves within the past two days. Kid Wade, Murphy, and Weatherwax were hung, while Hoyt and Old man Weatherwax were shot. Culbertson, Stewart, Morris and Cline are under indictment.[*] If the court fails to punish them the vigilantes will give them their attention. McFarland, who was captured and indicted, escaped. The cause of this summary work is the continued depredations by this Niobrara band of thieves. For years past they have operated with boldest impunity among the herds on this rich pastureland.
>
> The same band of thieves were formerly the famous

---

[*] Renamed Lexington
[*] Could this be the same Stewart who shot Schryer in Custer County?

highwaymen with Doc Middleton as their leader and when he was killed ** it was supposed the gang would break up and scatter. But, instead, it gained in strength and became more formidable than in the days of its notorious chief. The band finally reached such proportions that the law was absolutely set at defiance. They ruled the valley with impunity.

Last winter a meeting of stockmen and farmers was held for the purpose of organizing a vigilance committee to rid the valley of the terrible scourge. The committee gave desperadoes final warning a few months ago to leave the country. They disregarded the warning and the result is that ten of them are now under sod.

The courts would be beat out of more business and no one seemed to be too worried about it, least of all Gaslin and Dilworth.

In Sidney, Gaslin and his district attorney Dilworth impatiently awaited daily for the winter storms to abate. Day after day court was dismissed because of the weather. There was one case Gaslin was most anxious to try as the statute of limitation was about to release this character described as a "one-eyed wicked looking cuss." named Magrand. He was accused of murder on the McCann Ranch northwest of Sidney.

Beach Hinman of North Platte, defendant for Magrand, was urging trial. Witnesses from the McCann Ranch couldn't get in and without them, there wouldn't be much of a trial. Dilworth kept postponing the trial hoping that McCann and his cook, star witnesses to a contemptuous murder, could ride the 100 miles to reach court in time.

Finally Hinman approached Dilworth with a proposition: Magrand would plead guilty if Gaslin would agree to a sentence of ten years.

"I'll accept that plea," responded Dilworth and directed Hinman to make a deal regarding sentence. Hinman met with Gaslin and reported to Dilworth that Gaslin had agreed to the minimum sentence.

The next morning Magrand, with a huge chunk of tobacco in his mouth and his jaws working vigorously, appeared before Gaslin

---

** This is reported in error as Middleton died years later of natural causes in western Nebraska and entered a plea of guilty to murder in the second degree. Judge Gaslin pronounced sentence:

"It is the judgment of the court that you be taken from here to the penitentiary at Lincoln and there be confined at hard labor for the period of your natural life."

Murder gleamed from the eyes of Magrand, and Hinman jumped to his feet in a rage. The courtroom door opened and McCann and his cook entered, stamping snow off their feet.

Dilworth and the judge stared at the two for a moment, and then Dilworth said, "Mr. Hinman, if you desire to set these proceedings aside, the State will second the motion."

Hinman, realizing that Magrand would be convicted and maybe hanged if the plea were changed, responded quietly, "I believe we are ready to proceed with the next case."

A combination of events put a severe crimp in Print Olive's cattle business. As stated before, Judge Gaslin fined him $10,000 after the trial in Hastings, to pay the cost of the army sent to protect Gaslin and the court. Add to this the cost of several attorneys. The axiom of the range was that "if the court doesn't get you, your lawyers will."

Homesteaders had invaded his range until he had very little left, especially in Custer County. A blizzard winter struck and he had a tremendous "die up." After all this he was essentially bankrupt, or so it appeared.

He still didn't get along well with everyone and after he had an argument with Joe Sparrow over a small debt, he gave up and moved to Dodge City, Kansas with 4,000 head of mortgaged cattle.

CHAPTER SIXTEEN

IS THE FRONTIER CONQUERED?

From the <u>Western New Era</u>, April, l0, 1882---

> At the past term of court at Sidney, Judge Gaslin sent five men to the penitentiary. The judge is a terror to rogues and shyster lawyers. He has done good service in the Fifth Judicial District and commands the respect of and the confidence of all good citizens.

Judge Gaslin ate a late supper in a hotel-bar restaurant in Ogallala, arriving rather late on the evening train. He was tired and not looking forward to the heavy court schedule the next day. He planned to retire early.

He could hear cowboys in the barroom, getting noisier by the minute. He saw what looked like about fifty men as he walked through the barroom. They had been in town for several days, he was told, from the roundup and from one of the trail herds from Texas. The landlord sat down at Gaslin's table, a worried look on his face.

"I'm afraid we'll have trouble," he said. "Town's people are getting worried. They know what happens sometimes when cowboys get together."

He walked back to the barroom to hear screaming and yelling and some wrangling. The landlord came back.

"Every cowboy in the country knows you and respects you. Would you walk into the barroom and I'll let it be known you're here? That might settle them down."

The judge did as requested. As he walked in one man made a lunge at another with his fist, knocking him down. Others rushed to see the trouble just as a man who was down, came up, with a revolver in his hand. "I'll have fair play even if I have to clean out the room," he shouted and turned to his offender whose hand was on the butt of his revolver.

Several others drew revolvers. Soon there would be shooting. A man on the edge of the crowd noticed the judge. "Judge Gaslin, boys! The judge."

In an instance it was as quiet as death, said the reporter who wrote this story for his paper. Revolvers went into holsters and men who had been doing the loud talking were crawling out of sight.

One man, more self--possessed than the others, advanced and greeted the judge. Others followed. "Having a little fun, judge, that's all."

The judge tried hard to keep a straight face as the boys filed by. He had more trouble doing so when the man who threatened to clear out the room walked by. "Just having a political discussion."

The magistrate smiled as he said. "You know, if I had not come before you just as I did, I presume some would have come before me at this term of court."

"God forbid!" said one cowboy. "That is to say, sure don't want to."

The judge's appearance was magical. Five or six offered the Judge invitations to have a drink with the group.

The judge declined. But the rest of the evening, the boys were as quiet as kittens and not another word was heard even though they offered drinks to the old man's health many times, according to a New York reporter who was in town to account for any wild and woolly events.

In another event, the judge was holding court in a southwestern town. He had before him a man charged with a deadly assault but who had made out a good case of mistaken identity. He seemed likely to be acquitted. Judge Gaslin invited the jury to listen to the prisoner's answers to questions that he was about to propose.

The defendant turned pale. After swallowing a couple of times, he said: "That's all right, judge. If you're going to take a hand in this here thing, I'll cave. You needn't ask me any questions. I plead guilty and ask for mercy."

After sentencing the man to a long term in prison, he remarked: "I thought I would bring out a few points in case they would be of interest to the jury. I had advised him once before threatening this very man and I told him that he would get into worse trouble than this if he kept on. He thought I had forgotten him."

Sheriff Anderson, during one of his conferences with C. J. Dilworth and William Gaslin, reported on the final end for Print

Olive.

"I just got the news from the sheriff there. He was shot by a former employee who owed him $10."

Hard luck had plagued Print ever since the murder trial. His herds were decimated by the previous hard winter. The frontier telegraph indicated Ketchum's brothers were dogging his trail intending to kill him. And so he took his remaining cattle and moved to western Kansas.

He and other cattlemen pushed for a six-mile-wide cattle train from Texas to Montana, the same to be fenced. He helped established a new town on the Kansas-Colorado line west of Dodge City, Kansas and named it Trail City. There he built a saloon on the west side of Main Street. An old nemesis by the name of Sparrow built one on the east side. Sparrow still owed him $10 on a debt and Print wasn't polite in reminding him.

One day, as he was heading for his home in Dodge City, he walked into Sparrow's saloon to insist that Sparrow settle the account. Sparrow, so the story goes, met him with a blast from his .45 Colt and Print fell there in the doorway.

A friend rode to Dodge City to notify Mrs. Olive. She asked, "Was he carrying a gun?"

The man said "no."

"Just further proof that 'they that live by the sword, shall die by the sword,'" commented Dilworth.

"That six-mile wide trail is the last gasp of that Texas trail herd business, "added Gaslin.

In the Niobrara country Gaslin had a man before him charged with murder. The jury recommended mercy. The defense attorneys as well as the prisoner himself had made eloquent pleas to show that there had been great provocation. Judge Gaslin listened without emotion. Then, in passing sentence, he said, "I can take all things into knowing that shedding of human blood is a great evil but it sometimes happens to men and often cannot be avoided. I have known of such cases in my life and I am not prepared to say this case is not one of them.

"While the law is stern, it must be merciful, and nothing like vengeance is to be thought of. I feel justice in this case would be reached by imposing a sentence of the law that the prisoner be hanged by the neck until he is dead. I hope God will have mercy on him."

The shocked defense attorney jumped up, livid with anger. He raved, then concluded perhaps the court had absent mindedly passed sentence of death when his remarks logically tended to a less severe penalty

"The remarks of the court," insisted Gaslin, "are in full harmony with the law, and this attorney now before the bench will be imprisoned one day for contempt and for the logical results of his impertinence. Court dismissed."

For a time after the grasshopper years, during and after 1874, citizens dreaded crimes. As much as because it's perpetrators would have to be tried at considerable expense as they did the crime itself. Judge Gaslin gained fame for the economy with which he conducted court. Taxpayers groaned when they reflected that a trial had been to no purpose. When attorneys tried to secure a change of venue, new trials or postponements, it was of no avail. This judge held quick trials and sentenced the criminal if convicted and seldom allowed delays that cost poor counties more money.

He had two or three cases in a certain hard-up county. In one case attorneys for the man charged with stealing horses moved for a change of venue on the grounds that the people were prejudiced. The district attorney said that the cost to the people would be great if the case were taken to another county. Judge Gaslin said there was no occasion for removing it.

Then the counsel for the prisoner wanted a postponement. District Attorney Dilworth said "the jurors and witnesses are all here and it would involve considerable expense getting them together again."

"We'll have to proceed with the case," said Judge Gaslin.

A guilty verdict was rendered and a motion for a new trial was made and argued at great length.

Again Dilworth argued for no more trials. "The people are in beggarly condition and a new trial would cost a good deal of money."

"We will have to be satisfied with one trial this time," said the judge. "Everything seems to have been fair, and we must remember that the people have no money to waste on two trials when one will do just as well."

In another case, after a jury returned a guilty verdict and when there was a pressing need for expedition and economy Gaslin addressed the jury thus: "The case has gone before you, gentlemen. And you have found the prisoner guilty. I have no doubt of the prisoner's guilt and I presume you have not either. I have, however, some instructions from the prisoner's counsel, which desires that I should read to you. But I want you to understand right here that they are not good law." The instructions were read and still a verdict of guilt was rendered.

The judge was re-elected to a third term in 1883 but not with the same enthusiasm as the second. He had slipped into some bad habits such as too much freedom with the bottle, and it was hurting his reputation. Still, he won by a comfortable margin.

He was still held in high esteem by an eastern newspaper. The <u>Kearney New Era</u> weekly copied the following from the <u>New York Sun</u>, November 21, 1885. The reporter's lead paragraph read, "a model western judge. The terror of the cowboys and idol of peaceable citizens - his mode of giving justice."

The story continued:

A judge, whose circuit takes in about half of the state of Nebraska where there are few railroads and almost no conveniences, does not have an easy time of it, but he may be the very best kind of a magistrate. The man who deals out justice in the cattle country of Nebraska, holds court today in a town near Kansas, and the next day visits in a primitive court several hundred miles away in the direction of Dakota, must be energetic and industrious, and if at the same time administers justice promptly and at small expense, he will pass for a pretty good judge.

The frontiersmen of western Nebraska believe that they have such a character in Judge Gaslin, who has taken on the outlaws of the cowboy country for several years, and who promises to remain there as long as he lives. He has enemies among evil doers, as a matter of course, and occasionally a new attorney comes here with high notions as to things which are not in harmony with the old judge's views; but the great mass of the people, the men who own farms and who are trying to pay for farms and who want court expenses kept down to the lowest notch, are his staunch friends. The judge is not a believer in new trials, changes of venue or continuance, and when he gets hold of a criminal or civil case some end must be reached, and that is quickly.

He has established a reputation among cowboys that is the envy of other frontier judges and, though he is well along in years and could not make much of a fight himself, there is not a cow camp in western Nebraska where Judge Gaslin's presence would not immediately put everyone on good behavior. He is respected, as well as feared, and it has been said that his presence at an outbreak on the part of the boys anywhere would be worth more than that of a regiment of troupes.

The Fifth District was said, at one time "to be infested with some of the toughest gangs of lawless men, horse and cattle thieves, who congregated in one section of the country. Some had migrated from the extreme Southwest and even from Mexico." Judge Gaslin changed that.

His court business gradually slowed down after 1885. Accounts of murder, horse stealing and cattle rustling were noticeably fewer in number.

Another reason may have been a slow but sure change in the citizenship. Farmers and smaller ranches were slowly replacing the cowboys and the big cow outfits. Instead of open range, where the rule was "Who got there first, got the most", now land was coming under ownership with deeds and carefully defined section lines. Most good land had now been homesteaded. In ten years, the whole landscaped had changed. And in that change, Judge William Gaslin was all but forgotten in history books and in the memory of those living here. This concluded one of the most exciting times of that short decade.

Instead of murder cases the judge's work became more of settling boundary disputes, divorces, and other civil suits. A divorce case always brought sad memories of his failed marriage. What became of Catherine? If he knew, he never said.

Maybe the judge had a bad case of boredom, which caused him to drink more than he should. Besides fewer exciting murder cases, his far-flung Fifth District was divided into three districts and he became the judge of the Tenth District. His district now included most land south of the Platte River. He felt he had given up part of his life for the Fifth District where he had ruled with an iron hand, as far as the criminals were concerned. Maybe the criminals had something to do with getting him off the bench by creating new judicial districts.

The division infuriated Gaslin: "I covered the whole Fifth District by myself and had no trouble doing it. It was done just to make more room for more judges and it costs taxpayers more money. These new counties have enough trouble paying their expenses now."

But there was his drinking.

George L. Burr, editor of the <u>Register</u> in Aurora, told interesting anecdotes about the judge.

Burr was a boy freighter from Hastings to Smith County, Kansas. When on a return trip, he stopped over at Hunnell's Ranch between Hastings and Red Cloud for dinner. It was Election Day and the candidates were Gaslin and Dillworth. They had a good dinner, albeit considerably late. While they were eating with about a half dozen at the table, the little daughter of the proprietor, a five or six-year-old with long, beautiful curls, came to her father's arms and said, "They are having 'lection over at the schoolhouse, papa."

"Is that so, and did you vote?"

"Yes, I voted," she said.

"And who did you vote for?" inquired her father. "I voted for Dilworth. I didn't want no old Gaslin in mine."

"The man eating beside me ducked his head but never said a word," added Burr, "After dinner the other freighters told me it was Judge Gaslin himself and that he was a good judge.

Later, at Bloomington, Gaslin was holding court and Burr's father, E. M. Burr, was one of the attorneys at the bar. As the court was convening it became manifest that "His Honor" was very drunk and not fit to act on the bench.

"As father was bringing forward his case, the judge made a great effort to appear, with great pretense, attentive, but he as well as the onlookers realized that he couldn't conquer his disposition," said Burr.

"The court sojourned," enunciated Gaslin, thickly, "I'm not in condition to try a lawsuit and I'm not going to do it."

"To what date, your honor?" asked Burr's father.

"To the twenty-fifth of Deshember, said the judge.

"But, your honor that is a legal holiday."

Confusedly, he stared at the lawyers and jury. "Whatsh holiday comes on the twenty-fifth of Deshember?"

The judge gave up drinking a short time later, saying it is a disgusting habit.

"He was an influence for good," said the <u>Nebraska Bulletin</u>,

> "He acknowledged what was good, but sought to remedy what he believed to be wrong. He was a man of courage. He did not hesitate to condemn whenever he found that which did not accord with his ideals. He was the implacable enemy of wrongdoers. Yet, he had a heart that went out to the unfortunate."

This was not the typical viewpoint of most defense lawyers, though they respected him. They soon learned to depend on the Nebraska Supreme Court to get their clients out of jail, hoping to find a quirk in the law or a misstep by Gaslin in his zeal to see that a criminal was served justice quickly.

Said Virginia Falkner, in the University of Nebraska Press' <u>Roundup: A Nebraska Reader</u>.

> "Judge Gaslin contended that the way to put a stop to crime was by dealing out speedy, sure and severe punishment to confirmed and abandoned criminals and he had the nerve, strength, and iron will to execute the law without fear or favor. His unsophisticated, blunt, crisp way of running his courts and dispatching his business, while showing no favors, made many enemies among lawyers. The warden of the penitentiary considered him as one of their best suppliers.
>
> "The judge made the law to fit the crime and his methods struck terror in the hearts of lawbreakers, while it won the approval of the law-abiding members of the community and resulted in his re-election several times. When he ran for the second term, after civilizing and clearing the country of desperadoes and establishing law and order in four years, he had five votes more that the Republican and Democratic vote combined.

CHAPTER SEVENTEEN

THE JUDGE AND HIS GREAT NEPHEW

Many years later at nearly ninety years old, living in Omaha, John Haskell, the great nephew of Gaslin, wrote a biography titled **Judge William Gaslin, Nebraska Jurist** from which excerpts appear in this book with his permission.

Haskell states in conclusion in his book,

> *"I would like to inject my personal thoughts on conditions now as compared to the time of Judge Gaslin's career. According to his own words, he found his district in 'a reign of terror,' but with the able help of C.J. Dilworth they were able to secure conviction of the guilty and redeem the district from the lawless condition in which they found it."*

It would seem as though Haskell believed not much had changed as he wrote a diatribe in his book about the current day crimes and lack of punishment. He did not fault the police, but he does fault the judges and the public for not backing the judges who properly punish without delay.

Haskell held immense respect for his great uncle and enjoyed his countenance and his friendship. He described his great uncle as having "two fundamental principles: first, that strict justice must be promptly and properly administered, and second, that the equality of men must always be kept in mind."

Haskell stated that a move was made to elect Judge Gaslin to the Nebraska Supreme Court in 1879, which Gaslin turned down. So much for the accusation that he exploited the Olive trial as a way to get himself appointed to the Nebraska Supreme Court. In 1886 friends tried to get him to run for U. S. Congress but he showed no interest in that either.

Said the younger Haskell:

"*Although his court is best remembered for the criminal cases, there were also many civil disputes which he heard. A defendant in one of the judge's cases was being sued for non-payment of services. He had hired the plaintiff to plow or turn over the sod on a field of virgin sod.*

"After nearly an entire day of argument, getting nowhere, the judge declared a recess until the next morning. Gaslin, usually very prompt, was late for court, which caused much concern on the part of some of the staff. They were about to send someone to his hotel, thinking he must be sick, when he walked in and took his place at the bench.

"The judge announced the continuation of the case and said, "Gentlemen, I took it upon myself to ride out and personally inspect this job of breaking prairie. Anyone who would do such a horrible job does not deserve any compensation and he should be ashamed to ask for any. Case dismissed.'"

"As a young man," Haskell continued, "I had been under the impression that Judge Gaslin had many of his cases reversed by the Nebraska Supreme Court, I asked his friend, W. J. Furse, to explain. He replied that he thought that the number of cases was small in comparison to the number of cases that were tried in his court. The records show that of a total 278 cases, 157 were affirmed, 91 were reversed, five partially reversed and two dismissed."

But the judge was always upset when the Supreme Court reversed his cases and never hesitated to show his displeasure.

One case, which was upheld by the Supreme Court, occurred in a lawsuit in 1880. It had to do with the Burlington and Missouri Railroad's taxes for 1878 and 1879 owed to Kearney County. Gaslin's ruling for payment of $10,000 in taxes to the county was upheld by the high court.

Another case, upheld by the Nebraska Supreme Court, surprised the judge and others involved, including defense attorney, W. H. Thompson, who later became a Nebraska Supreme Court judge himself. It involved a fire insurance policy. Thompson argued persistently that the case should be tried by the court rather than by jury. When Gaslin agreed to this, Thompson felt confident he could win. However, the judge decided against the company and the case was immediately appealed.

While it was pending, Thompson met the judge on a train as he was returning from holding Court in Broken Bow. (Custer County was now in his district, thanks to a correction of the previous division by the state legislature.)

"May I ask you a question?"

"Yes."

"I was surprised at the judgment for the plaintiff after you stated the law was as I contended."

"Well, "said Gaslin, "the Supreme Court has been reversing when I knew I was right, so I thought I would just go them one better in this case and see what they would do with that."

Both were surprised when the Supreme Court affirmed his judgment.

Judge Gaslin vented his exasperation again after the trial of a man named Cook who had committed a horrible murder of his employer. The man was found guilty and was ready for sentencing. It should have been murder in the first degree, but before his trial a mob hanged and nearly killed him. The sheriff, who risked his own life to do it, rescued him.

When it came time to sentence the man the judge shouted out, "I'll tell you what I'll do. I'll give this man five years in the penitentiary if he and his attorney will agree that he take his medicine, or I will give him ten years in the pen and he can appeal to the Supreme Court and see what they will do for him."

Cook and his attorney quickly agreed to the shorter sentence and agreed not to appeal.

Gaslin's frustration with the justice system was vented in a speech at a murder trial in 1886.

"The moral sensibilities of the people are too often dead, and the laxity with which our criminal laws are enforced and criminals punished is to be deplored. Many jurors who look upon crime with such leniency are so easily wrought upon by the eloquent harangues of attorneys, that it is too often difficult to mete out justice.

"Reports of the decisions of courts of last resort in too many states evince a tendency to deal with form and legal technicality rather than substance. The humane view of the law for criminals - as it is so often called - so prevails in these modern days that it must seem to those of ordinary understanding who have seen many criminals escape, that there is a little protection for the people. In many places this feeling of uncertainty is bringing forth its fruits of lynch and mob violence.

"In one murder case, proceeding on error to the United States Supreme Court, the man was returned and incarcerated in

Buffalo County and let go after one of the greatest outrages and most dastardly proceedings ever perpetrated under the guise of legal form.

"I have not language to express my indignation and contempt for this transaction and those participating in it. After such a transaction, under so-called legal proceeding, who can blame the ordinary citizen unacquainted with legal technicality and proceedings for denouncing county officers and lawyers?"

As stated earlier, William Gaslin was judge of the Fifth District in the beginning, then judge of the 10th District as the number of districts was increased. Each time the subject came up; he opposed dividing into more districts, saying, "This is robbing taxpayers of nearly $100,000 annually."

To back up his viewpoint he added; "I kept my dockets clear and held court less than one-third of the time and had to travel by carriage to reach many of the courts, and had more criminal business than there was in any two other districts in the state.

"The first three years I was judge I tried twenty-six murder cases and the first six years, forty-three. In 1880, I held court in all of my districts in 130 days, the largest number I ever held in one year occasioned by an unusually large number of murder cases.

"Instead of increasing the number of judges and judicial districts, it would be better to enact laws requiring courts to open in the morning and run the entire day, and do an honest day's work, clear up the dockets and dispose of business thereon. If men in other vocations would run their business in the way many lawyers and courts do theirs, they would bankrupt themselves in a short time."

After sixteen years on the bench, William Gaslin's time as district judge ended in 1892, defeated by a candidate of the new Populist Party which was very strong during the 1890s among farmers. Theirs, as homesteading advanced across the state, became the dominating party.

It didn't make him very unhappy. The state had been divided into several more judicial districts, much to his disgust and against his advice. He had tamed the outlaws and the murder trials became fewer and fewer. He was ready for a change anyway. He opened a law office in Kearney and became Kearney's city attorney in 1896.

The <u>Omaha Mercury</u>, in Omaha, in 1902, ran an article

which shows how quickly man's memory fades in a short time:

> Judge William Gaslin, that has furnished a more vigorous and determined specimen of manhood and legal rectitude, is in town renewing acquaintances and attending to some business matters. The present generation has no recollection of the fearlessness of the days when as judge he carried his life in his hands as he sat on the misdemeanors of the lawless characters of this then new state.
>
> In those days he made himself a name that will descend in the history of the state as a man who, regardless of consequences, dealt out absolute justice to all as he saw it and, although often reversed in his courts in criminal cases, his sense of equity and justice was so keen that rarely were his decisions questioned by the bar or by the people. The judge still appears as a man who enjoys the good things of the world and the Mercury wishes for him many more years in which to enjoy life.

Other stories came along extolling his virtues and a few shortcomings among them:

A boy charged with stealing a horse that had been turned out to die. The boy had picked him up and rode to the next village and turned him loose. But someone charged the lad with horse stealing and he was hailed into Gaslin's court.

Gaslin questioned the boy, learning that he had come from an eastern state recently. "Do you have a mother?"

"Yes."

"Are you homesick? .... Yes."

"It is apparent to me that you are not "familiar with the ways of the West. I am turning you loose but I recommend that return to your home in the East and to your mother as quickly as possible."'

Gaslin had homesteaded in Harlan County and bought other land south of Alma. This country was always home to him. When the owner of the Harlan County Bank, Ed Willits, died in 1902 Gaslin bought it and moved there. He built a two-story brick bank building, which included his own living quarters. He hired Esker Cox of Hastings as vice-president and established a long-standing relationship that lasted the rest of his life.

And then came another example of his virtuous ways and

his belief in the goodness of man, if given a chance.

A farmer by the name of McKee had a feedlot full of cattle during the money panic of 1907 and the cashier in another bank said he couldn't extend his loan and he would have to sell the cattle and pay the loan.

He went to see Gaslin and told his story - how the market was so bad that if he sold the cattle now he would take enormous losses. "Mr. McKee," said banker Gaslin, "You just keep those cattle and sell them when they're ready." He did and paid off the loan to Gaslin's bank.

During one of his many visits to Maine, he invited his nephew, William Haskell, father of John, to leave his home and well-paying job in Maine to become a vice-president in his bank. He bought them a new home in Alma and included a room for his sister, Mary, to live in whenever she visited them.

He spent his latter years living with his nephew. During these years, he and his grand nephew became good friends and Gaslin often took him with him in his buggy to visit his farm and they had long talks. He had much contempt for idleness and wastefulness. He remained careless in dress, noted William Haskell.

The judge told his grandnephew, on one of his trips to his farms, that men who dress fancy were no good, "dam' dudes." But then proceeded to tell of the time he was visiting his mother in Maine. His mother had asked him to stop at the hotel kitchen to pick up her order. When his mother opened what he brought, she asked, "Will, where did you get this?" In it was a sandwich and some edibles. "I guess they thought I was a darn tramp," he replied sheepishly.

Coming with the Haskells was their young son, John. John's neighbor boy had a Shetland pony and he wanted one, too. His father refused to buy one.

The next day his Great Uncle Will came by, driving his beautiful bay Hambletonian horse, named Jim, hitched to his buggy with his faithful black and white Collie dog by his side. "Hop in." said his uncle.

There being nothing new about this, as his uncle did this often when he wanted to drive in the country to visit one of his farms or just pass the time and think. Or, he would talk over old times and reminisce, sometimes talking more to himself than to John. His huge frame took up a lot of the buggy seat and John looked sort of small sitting there squeezed in beside him.

John thought his uncle was going to one of his farms that day. Rather, he stopped at another farm. "Show us that horse you have for sale," said Gaslin.

The owner brought out a bay bronco-type mare with a couple of brands on her hip.

"What do you think of that pony?" asked his uncle. "Wouldn't you prefer that to a Shetland pony that is nothing but a toy?"

"Whee! You bet," shouted young Haskell.

Great Uncle Judge William Gaslin and John Haskell, Courtesy John Haskell

Back in town, Gaslin took John to the harness shop and purchased a new saddle and bridle. Gaslin thought it very important that John have a horse to learn to care for and appreciate the goodness of a horse to the betterment of one's life.

Haskell writes in his book, "As a judge, he was especially hard on horse thieves, and when asked why, he replied, 'When I lived at Lowell, the best and about the only friend I had was a white pony. It used to eat sugar of out of my hand and follow me about like a dog. Some d--- scoundrel stole him, and every time I sentenced a horse thief I would think of that pony and regret that there was limit as to the time I could send him up for." One wonders if he resented the fact he was never able to try and sentence Doc Middleton.

On January 14, 1910, Judge Gaslin failed to show up for breakfast. He had been staying with the Haskells lately.

Mrs. Haskell remarked to her husband. "Do you think something is wrong? You know he hasn't been feeling well for several days. William, go and see."

Haskell came back quickly. "He's breathing heavily and appears unconscious. I'll call the doctor."

The doctor examined the judge. "He'll breathe heavily for a time, then slowly stop. His time has come."

He died that evening at 5 p.m. at the age of 83.

The Haskells made funeral arrangements quickly and notified the local newspaper. The word spread rapidly of Gaslin's death with tributes to the good man pouring in from everywhere. A local headline read, "The foe of the cattle rustler, horse thief, murderer is dead".

The judge wasn't much for preachers and churches, although he never criticized them. However, the services were to be held in the Evangelical Church in Alma on Monday and J. P. A. Black of Hastings, a life long banker friend, was asked to deliver the funeral oration. He said:

"Nebraska in her short history, mourns the death of many great men -Gantt, Mason, Poppletin, Maxwell, Hitchcock, Furnas, Crounse, Thayer - but when the lapse of years shall have smoothed over a few rough surfaces, the candid judgment of the thinking people of the state of Nebraska will record the name of William Gaslin as peer among them all."

The <u>Hastings Daily Republican</u> paid Judge Gaslin homage in a long article about his life - how he homesteaded in Harlan County and was elected to the judgeship of the Fifth District. The newspaper recounted several incidents in his life but added one not reported in most newspapers:

> "A gruesome incident is related at the expense of the late judge. It is said that as he was coming to a town one day, while driving through a clump of low trees, a dry mummified body of an Indian that had been buried in the branches of a tree became loosened from its umbrageous sepulcher by the judge's wagon wheel striking the trunk of the tree, causing what remained of the Indian - dried skin and bones - to drop silently into the rear part of Judge Gaslin's wagon. It is said the jurist was so absorbed in matters of jurisprudence that he was not aware of the presence of the silent passenger who accompanied him in his conveyance until arriving in town, when he discovered the skeleton lying quietly in the rear end of the wagon box.

Judge William Gaslin's body was shipped back to Maine to be interred beside the remains of his mother and father and his sea captain brother.

Thus ended the career of a remarkable jurist. Haskell said in his biography of him "it is said that he sentenced more criminals to death and to the penitentiary than any man who ever sat upon the bench in the United States.

The tree Gaslin had planted in Lowell grew to be a tall shade tree and a blessing to the few persons still living there. It reminded him of his divorce but it also reminded him that life must go on. It grew to 90 feet tall and spread its branches over 100 feet, not unlike his stature.

"A wise king (or judge) stamps out crime by severe punishment" ---The Living Bible

Judge Gaslin Tree about 1875 – Its height was estimated at 90 feet, a giant Cottonwood and a giant man of his time.
  Courtesy John Haskell

Bibliography:

Books:

Butcher, S. D. *Pioneer History of Custer County and Short Sketches of Early Days in Nebraska*. Denver: The Merchants Publishing Co. 1901

Haskell, John. *Judge William Gaslin Nebraska Jurist.* Omaha: published by author 1983

Hutton, Harold. *The Luckiest Outlaw: The Life and Legends of Doc Middleton* by permission of the University of Nebraska Press. Copyright © 1974 by Harold Hutton.

Newspapers:
   Some newspapers have changed their name or are no longer existing, however these references are from the newspapers of the times.

Bloomington Guard, Bloomington, Nebraska
Daily Press and Dakotan, Yankton, South Dakota
Daily Press, Sidney, Nebraska
Indianapolis Sentinel, Indianapolis, Indiana
Hastings Daily Republican, Hastings, Nebraska
Kearney New Era Weekly, Kearney, Nebraska
Lexington Observer, Lexington, Nebraska (formerly Plum Creek)
McCook Weekly, McCook, Nebraska
Nebraska Bulletin, Lincoln, Nebraska
New York Sun, New York City, New York
North Platte Advertiser, North Platte, Nebraska
Omaha News, Omaha, Nebraska
Omaha Mercury, Omaha, Nebraska
Omaha Republican, Omaha, Nebraska
Omaha World Herald, Omaha, Nebraska
Platte Valley Independent, Grand Island, Nebraska
Register, Aurora, Nebraska
Red Cloud Chief, Red Cloud, Nebraska
Roundup: A Nebraska Reader, University of Nebraska Press, Lincoln, Ne
Wahoo Independent, Wahoo, Nebraska
Western New Era, Denver, Colorado

About the authors:

Roy Alleman was born and raised on a livestock farm in north central Nebraska, south of Loup City. He graduated from Wiggle Creek High School, and attended the University of Nebraska and Hastings College. He farmed early in life but later turned to journalism as a career. He has served as the editor of the Central Nebraska Farmer-Stockman of Cozad, the Custer County Chief in Broken Bow, and as farm editor of the Hastings Tribune, all in Nebraska. He is the author of the popular book **Blizzard 1949,** which chronicles the terrible blizzards and deep snows of on Nebraska winter. He also wrote **The Bloody Saga of White Rock**, about the first family to settle in northern Kansas. Roy passed away December 1999 at the age of 90. His wife, Irene, currently resides in Grand Island, Nebraska.

Carol L. Nowka was born and raised near Comstock, Nebraska, and graduated from Hyannis High School, Hyannis, Nebraska. She earned her Bachelor's degree from Hastings College and her Master's degree from Central Michigan University. She retired after 25 years as a Certified Financial Planner. She began a publishing company called Nebraska Wealth.com and began by reprinting her father's first two books. **The Judge, The Gavel, The Gun** is her first attempt at writing and publishing a book. Carol researched and added to the story regarding Doc Middleton.

CPSIA information can be obtained
at www.ICGtesting.com
Printed in the USA
LVHW021820170523
747246LV00004B/616